SAILING TO SCANDINAVIA

A JOURNEY TO THE END OF THE BALTIC SEA

FLORIAN JOHN HANAUER

Impressum
© 2021 Florian John Hanauer - All rights reserved

Edition Svanen

Text & Pictures: Florian John Hanauer
Cover: Panther Media / Carina Hansen
Logo: Swanest / Marcusw572 / Artpuppy (Moose)
Maps: openstreetmap.fr

Published by
Edition Svanen
Droste-Hülshoff-Str. 35
22609 Hamburg
Germany
www.edition-svanen.de

CONTENTS

FOREWORD

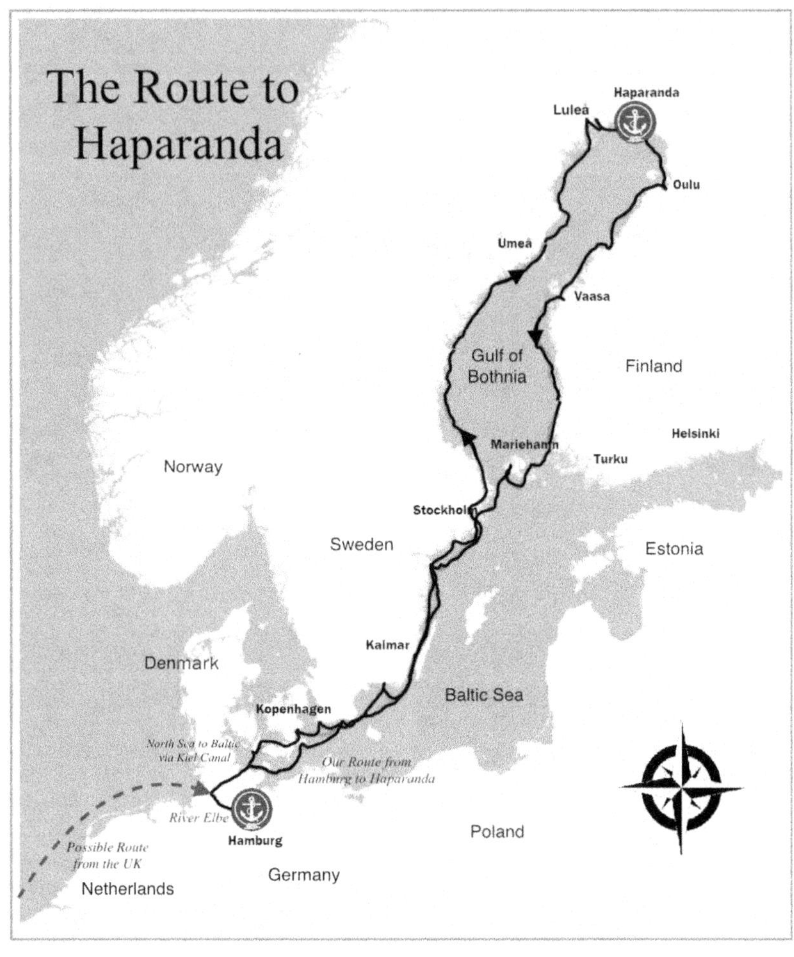

The route travelled in the summer of 2021

There is probably no other trip on the Baltic Sea as varied and long than sailing to Haparanda. The route stretches from the well-known sailing areas in Denmark and on the Swedish south coast to the archipelago of Stockholm. A third of the way from Germany to the Swedish capital passes through these island groups. But especially in the Gulf of Bothnia, where only a few recreational skippers are sailing: North of Stockholm, we continue to meander through small archipelago islands before we sail along the impressive High Coast, where the flat shore of the south gives way to small mountains. And then we arrive in the north, again between countless archipelagos to Haparanda. Finland, after all, is an exceptional sailing area, offering original destinations often hidden behind shallow waters.

Because there are so many different harbours on this route, we avoid longer strokes and call at no less than 70 harbours - from the big tourist ports to the enchanted fishing quay. This is also part of the charm of this route: Unlike cruises on the North Sea, the shore with its many skerries is usually never far away. Nevertheless, the trip is long, with several thousand nautical miles. The Bothnian Sea is much more versatile than I had previously thought. This had to become a book.

I started the manuscript with my sailing history on dinghies and yachts, which is not part of the trip to Haparanda. But I wanted to record how you get from dinghy sailing to cruising - just in case you've been wondering. Later I added the chapter about a visit to our homeport of Hamburg. That city is not in Scandinavia, really, but it's where we started and ended our trip. And if you are from the UK, from the Netherlands or Belgium, it might be an interesting destination by itself.

We like to sail a rather traditional boat with our „Vindö 32", with a long keel and a lot of wood in the superstructure and cockpit. Nevertheless, I think modern technology can be beneficial on board. However, as far as the gain in knowledge is concerned, I am sure that your horizons will constantly be broadened. You get to know foreign coasts much better when you sail towards them at a leisurely pace. I have garnished the book with practical tips from our sailing experience, which may be helpful at one point or another. There will always be different ways of doing this or that: you can go downwind to set sail, you don't have to. You can cook with kerosene, but you don't have to. I'm just explaining what I think works best on cruises like this.

Special thanks are due to my wife Birgit, who has enthusiastically lent a hand on this trip and was energetically at the tiller. And who later on supported the creation of this manuscript. But now I hope you enjoy reading it - maybe as much as I enjoyed writing it. Perhaps it will inspire you to go on a more extended voyage to Scandinavia yourself.

Hamburg, September 2022
Florian Hanauer

MEET MR. MOOSE

Hello, may I introduce myself? I am Mr Moose, the heraldic animal of Sweden, all of Scandinavia. I don't want to be too modest. After all, I am not an inconspicuous figure: I grow up to three metres long, and my shoulders can be up to 2.3 metres high. And I weigh 700 kilograms. I am an impressive animal, one that rests entirely within itself. My chest is big, and my shoulders are strong. But the most striking thing is my antlers, which are 1.30 metres wide. Apart from a few cheeky wolves or bears, I have no enemies.

I live up here in Europe in the Scandinavian forests, where I spend my days comfortably as a loner. Now you're wondering what I have to do with a book about sailing? Well, you may not know it, but we moose are good swimmers. When we think there are juicier tree shoots and aquatic plants on one of the many archipelagos, our favourite food, we swim.

And not exactly slowly: I can swim up to five knots in the sea. And I can swim long distances, too: I've already managed over ten nautical miles as a moose. I am quite an intelligent animal. That's why I'll calculate for you how fast that is in kilometres per hour: 10 times 1.852 makes 18.52 kilometres. Quite a distance, isn't it?

By the way, friends of mine have already swum from the Swedish mainland to the Aland Islands, as you humans have noticed. And because I always hear something about boats while swimming, I don't want to keep my tips to myself.

We moose like it cold. When the temperatures get too warm in summer, we feel uncomfortable. And when the flies and mosquitoes come along and get on our nerves, we retreat to the water. There we can cool down. And I can dive, too: I can reach depths of up to six metres underwater and can search the ground for food. You wouldn't have thought I could do that, would you?

Even though we usually roam the forests alone, we gather in communities in winter. We stand together and search for food in the snow. It's only in your cities, you humans, that we don't feel at home. There is far too much going on. I would love to wander through your pubs and try a beer. But we'd rather leave that territory to you. In this book I will guide you through the chapters. If you got any questions: You'll find us up in the north, in the next forest.

PROLOGUE

A TRIP WITH THE DINGHY TO DENMARK

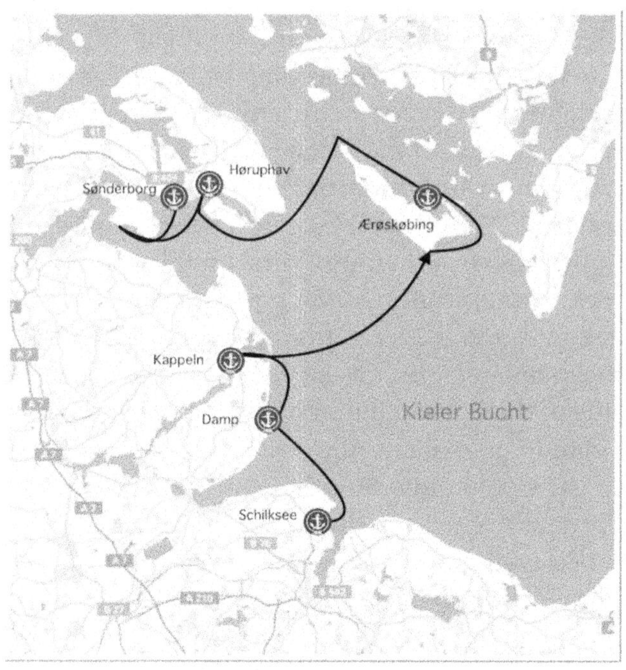

The bow of the dinghy cuts into the wave. Then the water lifts
the boat to crash over the small forecastle. The saltwater splashes
past the mast into the cockpit in a high arc. The light rainwear
can't do much to stop it. I'm soaked to the skin. Dinghy sailing is
generally a rather wet experience, but this can't go on for much
longer in the Flensburg Fjord.

The wind, which I'm cutting at a steep angle, is blowing far
too hard, the waves have already built up to a stately height at
just a few kilometres from the shore of the fjord. Above me, the
clouds are chasing across the sky. Diagonally to port lies the
harbour of Bockholmwik, across to the side the village of Lang-
balligau. That must be manageable, I think. It's not that far. I
have come as far as Denmark with the small dinghy, and now the
trip is supposed to end on the way back in the outer Flensburg
Fjord? But the weather is not impressed by such thoughts.
Nevertheless, the scenery seems almost unreal: At a distance of
one hundred metres, I see strollers on the beach waving, while
here I am fighting for every metre in the foaming fjord.

I travel by dinghy on the Baltic Sea. This marked the beginning of cruising because I went out from the inland lakes to the
sea. 15 years later, this should take me once around the Baltic
Sea. Everything went smoothly at first on this trip: From the
harbour Schilksee, I went via Damp to Kappeln. Then the
journey led to Denmark, once around the island Ærø. It went
back to the mainland, around the peninsula Kegnæs on the
Danish side of the fjord to the small town of Høruphav and
finally, it should go to Flensburg - all in about a week. A squall
shoots in. The Conger tilts precariously. I have to open the mainsail and lean far out to keep the boat from capsizing. The wind
tugs relentlessly at the jib and the mainsail. At least I make a
good speed. The beach passes quickly on starboard.

But again, a wave comes over and pours into the cockpit.
Everything is wet in the boat. I realize: This will probably not

work out. Then the decision is made quickly. I want to go back to Sonderburg just to get out of this white-water trip hard on the wind. At least I can turn the boat well in a wave trough. The boom comes over, the dinghy goes on course before the wind. That was off Gammelgab Strand on the Danish side of the fjord. I remember that place. Every time we will pass it later, I think back to it. Here the trip with a small, wet dinghy ended out of respect for the too big waves. Here, however, common sense prevailed over the ambition to reach a destination by sailboat at all costs.

The Conger dinghy ready to sail on a lake

After the turn, "Gorch Grog", as the Conger is called, begins to "surf". Not only does the strong wind drive him crossways from astern, but he goes down the wave crests. How fast I really am, I can't measure. There is no time to get out the cumbersome handheld GPS. Now concentration is needed to keep the boat under control. But the pace has to be fast. On the shore, the rotors of some Danish wind turbines are spinning feverishly. How pleasant the course downwind is all of a sudden, it flashes through my mind, compared to the arduous struggle against it. I round Kragesand and can sail along the peninsula in front of

Sonderborg. Suddenly the waves stop, the land covers the fjord, the water becomes calm. How is that possible, I ask myself: just now a brutal fight for every metre, now leisurely sailing? The sun comes out. I decide to head for the shore.

This is an advantage that no keelboat can offer. With the dinghy, you can easily take a break on the trip at the nearest accessible shore. I hoist the sails, pull up the daggerboard on its halyard and head for the shingle beach. On the beach in front of the forest near the village of Skelde Kobbel "Gorch Grog" comes to a halt. The wind rustles between the trees, but otherwise, it is quiet and relatively sheltered. Some holiday houses are standing on the shore, but no one is to be seen.

I take off the wet and useless rainwear. Unfortunately, the small cabin didn't stay dry. The breakers that kept coming over soaked everything: The blanket, the sleeping bag, but also the delicate handheld GPS, which wasn't really waterproof. With a "camping gas" stove, I can make a hot coffee and sit on the side of the boat. To the north lies Sonderborg with its marina. But before that, I see from the beach the Vemmingbugt, and here waves are piling up again. Even this smaller bay is enough to give the wind so much surface to attack that waves can build up. I feel like I'm in an obstacle course. I am already on the way back to Sonderburg, and just now, such obstacles must be overcome.

I decide to set off and make a wrong decision that could have had severe consequences: I want to cover the last stretch with the outboard to get into the harbour. The sail remains in the furling position above the Conger's boom. Today I know what a nonsensical thought that was: only the wind would have given the dinghy sufficient stability to get safely through the waves. But at that time, the marina seemed so close that it should be possible to get there quickly with the engine. At the same time, there was always the danger that the boat could capsize. Now, the Conger, with its 250 kilograms, is not lightweight for a dinghy, and this specimen also has the "Baltic Sea daggerboard", which adds an additional 30 kilograms of weight to the boat.

And at the top of the mast is a capsize cushion: an air cushion with a cartridge that strikes on contact with water and fills the cushion within seconds. The principle is the same as that of an automatic lifejacket. Because if the Conger capsizes, it would be pretty challenging to straighten it up again - especially with these waves.

Whether Baltic sword or capsize cushion, the possibility of a capsize remains. That's why I start the outboard. »Gorch Grog« sets off. In the Vemmingbugt, the waves slam sideways. The small outboard drives the dinghy bravely forward, but it starts to lurch violently with every breaker from the side. Now I practically learn that the danger for the boat without sails is much more severe. Almost unnoticed, a Danish rescue cruiser approaches on starboard. On this windy day, it has probably taken precautions to move into position in the bay off Sonderborg. Whether he sees me fighting here or not - it is reassuring to know him nearby.

But then it happens. With a crash, the waves hit hard, a strut of the small bracket of the outboard breaks. Now I have a problem. I can hold the motor on the right with my hand. On the left, a strut of the mounting still carries. Rather laboriously, I change course and head straight for the marina so that the wind only hits the boat diagonally from behind. Minutes later, I reach the pier of "Sonderborgs Lystbadehavn". Another crash, the outboard's bracket finally breaks off, right in front of the outer jetty. Some sailors have watched the approach. I heave the outboard into the boat with a big swing, which was about to disappear into the harbour basin. Someone throws me a line, I can pull the dinghy to a bollard. Helping hands grab it from the jetty and moor the Conger to the fore and stern lines.

"Gorch Grog" lies on the jetty with a defective bracket but otherwise undamaged. Everything is wet, including the clothes in the cabin. But in the clubhouse in Sonderborg, a hot shower is waiting for the skipper and a tumble dryer to dry the completely soaked garments. "What happened to you? Did you fall into the dock?" A woman looks at me, somewhat stunned as I stand dripping wet in front of the clothes dryer.

"No, no, I was out there," I answered her, pointing toward the sea.

"You went out with this weather forecast? And have a yacht sailing so wet?"

Wet sailing is already technical jargon, meaning that you get wet in your boat while sailing.

"Well, it's a dinghy, and you sail wet," I reply. The woman is astonished.

"You sail in a dinghy in this weather. So never would I do such a thing. We'd rather sit in our warm cabin." Shaking her head, she leaves the laundry room.

I'd also like to sit in a warm cabin now, just that "Gorch Grog" doesn't have an actual cabin, and it's not warm anyway. Rather a little wet, as the whole dinghy sails wet.

A little later the owner of a large yacht passes by "Gorch Grog".

"I can't stand by and see you standing here in front of your dinghy. I've made you a pot of hot water," he says.

Then he offers to fix me the outboard bracket. "Yes, but how", I ask, "I can fix that in my onboard workshop."

I follow him into the cockpit of his yacht. "The bad weather continues", he says, "the barometer is still dropping." I'm stunned, not just by his barometer and the big ship. He actually has something like a workshop below deck. He can shorten a metal strut and drill holes into it so I can screw it to the broken bracket.

"It's a temporary fix," he says, "but one that will probably last a long time." True: Even today, when the Conger has long returned to an inland lake, the bracing on the stern is holding. I'm impressed and resolve to be just as helpful to other sailors when they encounter me with problems.

Sailing started for me with dinghies on inland waters. The first boat was an old Danish "Hjerter" dinghy. This construction from the sixties was one of the first sailing boats made of GRP. I did self-experiments on the lake with friends because none of us could sail properly. After several attempts, which often ended in the reeds on the opposite side of the lake, we had the boat reasonably under control. "Hard to sail, but pretty fast," was my sailing instructor's later verdict on the "Hjerter". But because the shrouds were no longer in order and the mast was damaged, a replacement was needed.

The Conger seemed the best choice: From the beginning, the small "slip cabin" appealed to me to go on tour later on. I dreamed of putting it on a lake or even on the Alster, right in the middle of Hamburg. The previous owner had bought "Gorch Grog", the name remained unchanged, to sail with it on the Saaler Bodden on Germanys Baltic coast. For this reason, he had also equipped it with the heavy daggerboard.

When I was drawn to the sea, I had already discovered that boats can be used not only for sailing in circles or racing but also for sailing to distant destinations. The realization matured during a stay in the US. No wonder we were in Newport, a sailing mecca on the East Coast. For a few days off Newport, my wife Birgit and I sailed with a "Rhodes 19", a 5.80 meter long, small keel yacht. Of course, this beautiful area contributed to my enthusiasm for cruising. Off Rhode Island, we headed for bays, crossed waters and moored in other harbours. The northern US east coast reminds me of our Scandinavian sailing grounds.

The first time there was a good wind, it must have been around five to six Beaufort. We had reefed the mainsail quite rustic and tied it around the boom. The sailboat owner was cruising the bay in his motorboat and also came alongside twice. "Are you all right?" he asked anxiously. Yes, we had no problems in this boat. On the other side of the bay, we moored in front of a coffee shop to take a break. That worked out well.

The second time it went less smoothly after casting off because we got too close to the coast and promptly grounded our little keelboat. The harbour master had to tow us free with his motorboat, which he managed well with a grin. There it was, the helpfulness among the sailors, who taught us a lot about the "Rhodes". The US sailors seemed to me to be more uncomplicated. They had a less formal, shirt-sleeved manner that I liked. There was no elitist posturing along the lines of "I know something you don't know", but a friendly, hands-on "Let me show you how it's done".

Back in Germany, there was still no stopping us. We had already sailed on the Baltic Sea when I had passed the "Sportbootführerschein Binnen", the basic german sailing license. So I planned a trip from Schilksee on the coast to Flensburg, which no longer seemed unrealistic. The Conger is a rather heavy dinghy. It has a tiny cabin in front of its cockpit, which the shipyard has called a "slip cabin", probably because you are supposed to slip into it. It's a little bigger than the Rhodes 19. Theoretically, it would provide a berth for two adults if you moved together, had no luggage at all or completely emptied out the cabin. And if it were dry - which it seldom is due to the daggerboard box, which is only sealed at the top by two rubber strips.

The dinghy was quickly loaded onto a small trailer from a shallow part of the lake and brought to the Baltic Sea. In the harbour of Schilksee, the boat lay there and was equipped: All kinds of provisions went into the small cabin, life jackets, waterproof shoulder bags, and an outboard motor that fit on the bracket at the stern. I was particularly proud of the waterproof bag for the mobile phone, in which it could even still be operated with its buttons, which I tried out. With today's smartphones with their "touch display," this is no longer possible in the water.

Together with a friend, I sailed off at the beginning of June. First, we went to Damp, the holiday resort that used to be called "Damp 2000" until the name became unfashionable when the year 2000 was over. What a feeling! The harbour was not crowded. We could tie the dinghy to the thick posts at the guest jetty. From Damp, we sailed on to Kappeln. Between big yachts, "Gorch Grog" pushed up the Schlei. We felt like circumnavigators. In Kappeln, we took a lot of time for the manoeuvre to moor all lines correctly in the town harbour.

"What are you sailing in?" the harbour master asked us. "That's a Conger we're sailing along the coast with," I replied. "Along the Schlei?" he asked. Well, that would have been nice too. But I explained to him that we were on our way to Flensburg. "In that little boat? No one has done that for a long time. There was one like that a few years ago," he replied. "If you're going to pull this off - I just can't charge you a harbour fee."

Because the weather was stable, light winds were blowing, and the sun was shining, I decided to take a short detour to Denmark. From Kappeln via Schleimünde, I should go to Ærøskøbing on the east side of the Danish island Ærø. That went well, even though it was a bit of a queasy feeling when the land went out of sight on the small dinghy, and only a pocket compass pointed the way. But the sea was peaceful, and after a few hours, "Gorch Grog" was able to take a break on the island's beach under three windmills.

The first navigation experiences followed immediately: Behind Marstal, the water becomes relatively shallow. Keelboats have to take a bow to the northeast on their way to Ærøskøbing. But even a flat-bottomed conger with a slightly retracted daggerboard has problems with draught on the direct route between Marstal and Ærøskøbing. I had to steer the boat once around the island of Halmø. I could clearly see the sandy bottom, and there was enough draught left. Done: "Gorch Grog" came to Ærøskøbing. In a small dinghy, let it be understood, that was the distance of about 33 nautical miles in one day.

The experience was also hearty: meals were served on the beach. The Conger was pulled up for this. Then the "camping gas" stove was unpacked from the cabin, and cans were heated in the pot. For the nights, we occasionally helped ourselves with a little trick: due to some overnight stays in hotels, the nights were by no means as spartan as the inventors of the "slip cabin" had obviously had in mind. A real bed was better than the damp and cold mini-cabin. It felt like a perfect combination: Travelling by dinghy, close to the water. The nights were a bit rustic on the beach, but also comfortable in inns and hotels. However comfort or not: Ærøskøbing, this beautiful Danish sailing harbour, where the dinghy had a fine spot in the port, was so impressive that I hardly felt like leaving the place in search of an inn. How nice would it be to not only moor the dinghy here but to be able to stay onboard the whole time?

The last scheduled stop on the way back from Ærø was Høruphav, just before Sonderborg. Directly at the marina is the beautiful Hotel Baltic. There, even haggard sailors who have crossed the Little Belt in a dinghy can spend the night. Here the weather changed at the same time. The bright sunshine turned into dense and then dark clouds the next morning. Instead of the light breeze, a stiff wind blew. The leisurely glide at three knots turned into a fast ride, from Høruphav past Sonderburg into the fjord - and then back to Sonderborg.

It seemed like a great adventure to me. And I had not read Peter Clutterbuck's book with the promising title "The Sea Takes No Prisoners: Offshore voyages in an open dinghy" until much, much later. He managed to sail from Great Britain to Norway in a small sailboat. If I had known it then, I probably would have set off on further adventures with the Conger.

But after this trip, it was clear that I needed a small yacht, also called a "pocket cruiser". A keelboat, at least big enough to withstand waves like those on the Flensburg Fjord. After the Conger, which I still have, by the way, two keelboats followed, a Kelt 620 and a Jaguar 25, until my wife Birgit and I finally bought the Vindö 32, with which we set off around the Baltic Sea years later. And because my job as a journalist took me to different cities, we also sailed in other areas because the boat always came along. After the western Baltic, we sailed in the waters of Berlin, on the Spree and the Wannsee. We sailed across the Oder to the Polish coast and to Bornholm. Later we went to Bremen, on the Weser. From Bremerhaven, we sailed to the Wadden Sea and the

East Frisian Islands. Finally, we returned to the western Baltic Sea and undertook trips up to the Kattegat, to Gothenburg and further into the Skagerrak. Later we also got to know the Netherlands, France and the British coast.

Today I would say about the trip with the Conger: It was an adventure, in parts also a somewhat daring one. It is possible to sail across the Baltic Sea with a dinghy. However, you should avoid strong winds. To counter the waves, you need a specific size of boat. It is better to gain experience with a small keelboat on the Baltic Sea and other coasts.

1 DEPARTURE: FROM HAMBURG TO THE NORTH

A journey to the end of the Baltic Sea begins by heading for the Baltic Sea. If you are starting from Denmark, the German Baltic Coast, or Poland, you are already there, and can simply head northeast. But if you're coming from Hamburg, like us, you have to get there first. Either through the Kiel Canal or the Elbe-Lübeck Canal. From Berlin, the options are similar: there are also two routes, one via the Oder-Havel Canal to Szczecin and then into the Baltic Sea, or the long route via the Mittelland Canal and Elbe-Seiten Canal and Lübeck to Travemünde. Sailors coming from the Weser or the Ems do not have to think long and head for Cuxhaven and the Kiel Canal.

The same is true for anyone sailing from the Netherlands, from the UK, Belgium and France or maybe even from overseas. It all goes through the Kiel Canal. Of course, theoretically there is still the route to sail up the Danish North Sea coast and then via the Limfjord or around Skagen into the Kattegat and the Baltic Sea. But that would be a trip in its own right, not a feeder trip like we are planning.

So if you want to get through the canal into the Baltic Sea, you have to reach the river Elbe. Two places will be important for you: Cuxhaven, which lies at the exit of the Elbe into the North Sea, and Brunsbüttel, where the canal begins. Now maybe a detour to the island of Helgoland, right in the middle of the German bight, is worthwhile if you are coming from Western Europe. That would be a port where the tidal current is not yet so strong and where you can get provisions cheaply. After that, with a good wind, you can reach Cuxhaven in a few hours.

But be warned: the current in the Elbe estuary can take on considerable proportions. I remember well how we once tried to enter the Elbe against the current. On the way out of the Wadden Sea, I needed time until the tide came in and so much water runs into our little harbour again on departure that "Svanen" floated again. Before, she was sitting on the soft silt. But this drags on for the whole morning. Actually too late, I could safely cast off without getting stuck in the harbour right away. Up to „Scharhörnriff" it was a very fast trip: fresh wind blowed from the right direction, all sails were up, I got to a speed of 6.8 to 7 knots through the water.

But that was the speed through the water, not over the ground - a distinction that is essential in tidal areas like the North Sea. So: "Svanen" was only travelling at five knots over ground, because the tide was now flowing well into the German Bight. I could observe the seven knots on the log and enjoy this rather theoretical value. But all the same: if I only made six knots through the water, there would only be four left over the ground.

Up to Scharhörn it all still works. When I turn onto the Outer Elbe, I passed a hydrographic research ship in the beautiful sunshine. Its dinghies, the "Komet 2" and "Komet 3", scaned the sandbanks in long loops to measure them.

This was followed by heavy shipping traffic on the Outer Elbe, in the direction of Cuxhaven, but also out to sea. Tankers passed us, container ships, some of them really big, even the Helgoland ferry steams past. The strip next to the actual fairway is so wide that a sailing boat can still sail there and not even come into contact with the fairway between the red and green buoys. Unless you have to cross.

But the wind direction is still right, I can continue sailing with „Svanen" on the „Außenelbe". But what was that? When the island of Scharhörn with its sandbanks appeared on starboard, the current became stronger. Now it was against me at 2.5 knots. What was that still doing over ground? Well, there are still 3.5 knots left.

The current increased, more and more water flowed out of the Elbe into the open sea. Behind Scharhörn it was first 3, then 3.5 knots against on. I had to start the engine to help it along. So I got back up to seven knots through the water, but only 3.5 knots remained. In moments like this, of course, there's no need to discuss whether to sail or to use the engine - you simply need everything that makes speed.

It was getting dark, the sun was preparing to set over the horizon in the west. The ships had already switched on their position lanterns. There is supposed to be a place in the mudflats where skippers who can no longer make it against the tide to Cuxhaven could spend the night. To moor safely in a tidal flat, that would be something. But Cuxhaven already appeared in front of me, it seemed within reach.

As if the Elbe had foreseen this, as if it wanted to give me a particularly tricky task: it turned up, first it was 4.5 and then a full five knots of current. Of my beautiful seven knots, only two remained. A few minutes later I'm only doing 1.6 knots over the ground. How long would it take to reach the safe harbour? The plotter knew the time of arrival on the route: 10.30 p.m., although it was only 7 p.m. and land seemed so close.

When sailing on the North Sea, you simply have to "reconcile" a lot of factors. On the Baltic Sea, you are primarily concerned with the weather, i.e. the wind strength, the wind direction, the wave height and perhaps whether it is raining or dry.

There was too little wind for sailing now, and the direction of travel was right into the wind. Crossing in the fairway in the dark, that was not necessary. I hoisted the sails: the furling jib was simply rolled up, the main fell onto the boom and is lashed there well. I had to increase the revs from the diesel, then it still manages to bring the boat up to 6.8 knots.

Hour after hour passed like this on the Outer Elbe. Finally, the guide dam off Cuxhaven was over and the Kugelbake appeared on the starboard side. But it was hardly visible: All you could see was a dark scaffolding jutting up into the night sky. In between, some visitors twinkled around with their torches, which could be a bit irritating on the water. I was glad when I passed the spherical beacon in the middle of the rushing water.

Now it was only a short distance to the marina, just behind the ferry terminal. That passed too, here on the dark Elbe. It was eerie once again to turn into the entrance to the marina in the strong current. I swung the rudder around, the ship turned in and suddenly the current eased.

I sailed along the jetties until a friendly sailor from the Netherlands pointed to a place: „Here is still free", he called, and helped to take the lines. The Vindö was quickly moored, at the floating jetty on the side and in front. The ship was moored. It had actually become 10.30 p.m.

Well, this little episode will not be unfamiliar to sailors coming from the British, Belgian or Dutch coasts, as well as from France. I just wanted to remind you that the Elbe can also develop a powerful current. Remember: we had five knots of current against us. The smartest way would be: Be at the Scharhörn reef in time with the rising water if you want to enter the Elbe from the west, because the current gets stronger there.

But the trip through the Wadden Sea and into the Elbe is very beautiful, I can assure you. Behind the islands you can sail nicely to the east (if the draught is not more than, say, 1.40 metres, otherwise it's better to sail around the outside). And the Netherlands is also a great sailing area. But in the Baltic Sea, "tideless fun" awaits us, and that's why we're now moving on to this sea area.

Our destination is the Gulf of Bothnia, the sea area north of Stockholm on the Swedish side and north of Turku on the Finnish side. We want to sail around it. Thus, it goes beyond the "actual Baltic Sea", as it is correctly called, as the Gulf of Bothnia does not belong to it.

In view of the great distance we are running out of time, even if we could take time off: For me, and then for my wife, the career break worked out after all. But now I'm calculating: June, July and August are available, maybe September too. But in autumn I would like to have left the far north again - which should turn out to be right later. While the sailing season is still in full swing here in northern Germany, the guest harbours in central and northern Sweden close at the end of August. In autumn you can still sail in the "southern" latitudes of our north, but up there the season is then over.

The first stage is supposed to be via the Kiel Canal to Fehmarn. I actually like the Elbe-Lübeck Canal better: it's a wonderful blue ribbon that runs through the hilly landscape of East Holstein, interrupted by small locks and without much commercial shipping. It is also shorter than the route via Bruns-büttel into the "big canal". But it has a decisive disadvantage for a half-grown sailing yacht: the mast has to be laid, otherwise there is no way through under the numerous bridges. Already at the Elbe bridges in Hamburg the trip would be over if the mast is not laid. Now there is an excellent mast crane in Travemünde in the Passat harbour, with which we could put it up again.

But since the mast is already well adjusted to "Svanen", the shrouds all have a finely tuned tension, we do not want to take it down again immediately. This was different with our previous boat, the Jaguar 25: It had a device near the mast, a large "V" out of stainless steel, with which you could lay and set the smaller mast quite quickly. In about two hours the manoeuvre was perfectly done, without any aids. But on "Svanen", with its mast height of 12.70 metres, this is no longer so easy.

Of course Hamburg, our home town on the Elbe, is worth a visit and also has a very attractive marina. There is more about that at the end of this book. You could sail in there via the Elbe while you're here.

The idea of a trip to Haparanda had been haunting my mind for a long time, after we had made trips to the Kattegat and Skagerrak from the western Baltic and also sailed to Born-holm and the Polish coast. But now for once a really long stretch of sailing, with lots of unfamiliar places, always close to the coast. Visiting Stockholm, the Åland Islands and the Finnish coast. What would it be like on the shores of the Bothnian Sea? Are the thousands of archipelagos in Finland an attractive sailing area? What would it be like to reach the northernmost buoy in Norbotten? The wording of "Hamburg" and

"Haparanda" makes a nice double sound, so it became the title of this book.

And there is another question that I am bothering with: What is it actually like with the moose in the far north? In a TV report about northern Sweden, we had seen that the moose swim back and forth between the archipelago islands. And you can also see numerous videos of swimming moose on Youtube. Now, I really would like to see Mr Moose in the wild and maybe even from a boat, too.

But the time frame was very tight: First of all, the boat had to go to Stockholm, because at the end of June there was also a change of residence. So there were about 16 days left for the journey. Let's see how far we can get "Svanen" in this time. Up to Fehmarn my wife goes along, afterwards I want to bring the boat further single-handed. At the beginning of July, so the plan, Birgit and I then want to return and start the journey from Stockholm around the Bothnian Sea.

INFO: THROUGH THE CANAL

It has its advantages, the almost 100-kilometre-long canal that connects the Elbe at Brunsbüttel with the western Baltic Sea. Anyone who has ever travelled the dead-straight "Mittelland Canal" that cuts through northern Germany will quickly come to appreciate the "NOK": Compared to the inland waterways, it is wide and spacious. It is true that sailing is prohibited here, the engine must always be running, even on a sailing yacht. But sails may be set for support. And the mast can remain standing. Those who plan to pass the 98.6-kilometre-long canal in one day with a sailing boat could get quite sweaty: Because pleasure boats are only allowed to navigate it during daylight. It is better to plan a stopover in advance. For this, the branch of the Giselau Canal is a good place to moor, directly in front of the Giselau lock. Or of course Rendsburg, where you leave the canal into the Ober-Eider-See and have a choice of several sailing clubs on your port side. We always chose the one at the back, which is closest to the city. Because the centre with good restaurants is only a short walk away from there. A stop at Flemhuder See, north of Westensee, where you can moor at dolphins or buoys, is also original. What else is there to consider? At both entrances and exits of the canal, there are sport boat maintenance stations. There you can simply listen to channel 13 (at the west end) or channel 12 (at the east end) with your VHF radio. Usually there are already so many sailors in the waiting area that you can join them and sail into the lock with them. This is allowed when the lights at the entrance are flashing white (the green signal is only for commercial shipping). Mooring to the pontoons, which rise and fall with the water level in the lock, is straightforward: The mooring lines are looped around iron rings at the front and back and, thanks to the floating pontoons, remain taut. You just have to be careful not to slip on the wood. During the canal trip, one should drive at the starboard side of the bank, as often really big professional ships pass. And if a traffic jam forms, before the entrance at a so-called switch, then please also wait behind the last ship and do not overtake the big ones. And the payment? There are pay machines for that at the waiting areas on both sides. Incidentally, during the Corona pandemic, the obligation to pay was also suspended for pleasure boats.

Mr Moose says: *I have heard about this canal. It is supposed to be a fast connection to the Baltic Sea. But it's too crowded for me down*

there. There are people, cars, boats and big ships everywhere. Make sure you get through it as fast as possible and quickly reach my territory up here.

As soon as the lock gates of the canal open, the exit into the western Baltic Sea is free. From Hamburg with the outgoing water we went to Glückstadt, then via Brunsbüttel into the canal, an overnight stay in Rendsburg. In the western Baltic Sea the first stop could be the Marina Wendtorf, or the harbours of Laboe as well as Strande. Wendtorf is packed with yachts on this June evening.

The harbour is a huge facility that shows its past. Scenically, it lies extremely charming behind the nature reserve Bottsand. The beauty is no wonder, at the beginning of the nineteen seventies, a large part of this nature reserve with its lagoon had been built. In the eighties and nineties, the resort and its small shopping centre visibly deteriorated, the swimming pool disappeared. The marina is surrounded by high-rise buildings in concrete construction of the seventies, real „storey construction". It was only a few years ago that some momentum was created with new, smaller houses. Nevertheless, the new holiday flats close to the quay seem a bit out of place. However, the jetties of the harbour were also redeveloped quite leisurely. Instead, the shopping centre including a good Italian restaurant was simply demolished. It's going slowly, the crumbling concrete of the harbour master's office testifies to that.

In the lock of the Kiel Canal

Small annoyance: The cumbersome deposit card, which must be purchased in addition to the 20 euros mooring fee for the use of the sanitary facilities. Since the next morning the machine is on strike at the return, I can only throw it in a mailbox and do without the payment of the deposit.

But the next day, just east of Wendtorf, we had a very special experience: The Todendorf training area is a shooting range. In the context of a NATO exercise, the entire sea area on the coast is closed, which is not so rare. You can find this information on the net, in the sea weather forecasts of dp07 or it is announced on channel 16 on marine radio. In such cases you have to sail a detour, because the training area of the German Armed Forces reaches almost to the Danish sea border. The way to Fehmarn thus becomes five nautical miles longer.

So we take course to the northeast, although we actually want to go directly east. Every minute the announcements come: The navy warns ships to leave the shooting area. Some answer, many do not answer and are radioed several times. This is amusing until the name of our boat sounds from the loudspeaker: The navy asks me to leave the training area immediately. Completely baffled, I promise to run off to the west while looking outside at the barrels of the restricted area. I am sure that I have not entered the training area.

But five minutes later „Todendorf Radio" reports again: Why we had not left the shooting area despite being asked to do so, the radio operator, who was already a touch more unfriendly, want to know. „We are definitely not in the shooting area," I answer, „but outside, I see the buoys to starboard." He then asks me to put through my own GPS position. Lo and behold, suddenly the voice becomes friendlier. „We're having some problems with our equipment," the radio operator explains. The position had been determined incorrectly. Well, it can happen. But shouldn't the Navy be able to determine positions clearly? Are these now the effects of the austerity measures in the Bundeswehr? After this incident, the journey to Fehmarn is sunny and brisk. But all the next day, already far in Denmark, I hear the calls of „Todendorf Radio" on channel 16, which incessantly warns ships to leave its warning area and obviously has an excellent range.

The journey towards Stockholm continues quickly. In Fehmarn Birgit unfortunately has to leave the ship, because her summer vacation has not begun yet. So first of all I sail „single-handed" further, which means in the „sailor slang" simply alone. Because the skipper needs one hand to hold on and one to sail. I had planned a „60", a distance of 60 nautical miles a day, which should lead me past Gedser along the Hjelm Bay to Klintholm.

Only the wind is missing, the sea is as smooth as glass. So „Svanen" steams ahead under motor, on deck a Bruce Spingsteen concert is playing. „Real" sailors on the Baltic Sea always say that they don't like to sail under engine. Nevertheless, an astonishing number of them do, even though we have a boat whose main propulsion is the sails. But with a distant destination in sight and no wind, I turn a blind eye. Especially as the Volvo Penta diesel on „Svanen", a replacement engine from 2015, is really doing an excellent job.

Klintholm is a beautiful harbour, which I remember from pre-Corona times as always well visited, if not overcrowded. It's right by the impressive cliffs of Mön, the counterpart to the Rügen chalk cliffs further south. When we bought „Svanen" in Denmark three years ago, this was the first harbour we called at. And almost as if on order, Swedish sailors passed by the jetty, admiring the ship and raving about the times when they themselves still sailed a Vindö. But now, at the beginning of June, the harbour is almost deserted. The harbour masters Michel and Bente Larsen are in charge of the guest harbour. They don't check the papers, even though I had gone to Germany to get a Corona test. „We trust our guests," says Bente Larsen. Why is there hardly anything going on, I ask. „Yes, the season is getting off to a slow start," the harbour master replies. Already next week it will be fuller. The place looks deserted.

The next day, another „60" is on the agenda: In one go from Klintholm to Ystad in Sweden. Leaving the cliffs of Mön behind me, I have to steer into a field of fog to avoid the wind farm between Denmark and Sweden. It looks spooky: While the tips of the wind turbines stick out of the fog, everything on the water surface remains in dense grey. I do my best to avoid the route of the ferries on their way to Trelleborg. Suddenly, a grey shadow appears to starboard: A Swedish naval vessel is approaching, sailing exactly on the sea border with Denmark. Unlike the German Navy, the Swedes do not even emit an AIS signal. That would at least have made the ship appear on the plotter. So the grey monster passes directly in front of my bow, only to disappear again in the fog. The encounter is finally scary, but uncomplicated. As a kind of reward, the wind comes up, first with three Beaufort, then with four. Perfect, I quickly hoist the mainsail and unfurl the foresail, the genoa. „Svanen" picks up speed. The weather is clearing and the Swedish coast is rapidly approaching.

When I reach Ystad at 17:30, I am amazed, first on the jetty in front of the harbour master, then in the town: Nobody wears any mask here. Nobody keeps distance or uses the dispensers with hand disinfection in front of the shops. Of course, you could read before how liberally Sweden handled the Corona crisis in the summer of 2021, but witnessing it is something else. If I was not vaccinated, I would no longer feel completely safe and calm.

From Ystad it goes again through a Swedish firing range, which was fortunately not in operation, to Simrishamn. The harbour master had reassured me before: No, there are indeed exercises in a shooting area, as I had read online. But this is a different one, in the direction of Karlskrona. The southern coast of Sweden resembles ours with its sandy beaches and long pine forest. Simrishamn is a convenient, large guest harbour with finger pontoons replacing the cumbersome stern piles that are common in the south of the Baltic, but which you don't encounter at all further north. And I have arrived in high-tech land: While in Germany there are still harbour masters who collect mooring fees, in Denmark vending machines, here in Sweden for the first time it is only possible via app. Even the electricity must be activated via a small keypad on the pillar on the jetty with a pin code that you get online. Actually practical, I think, until I notice the desperate attempts of a German couple, who do not get along with this system at all. They are a bit older and sail the same route with their Najad as I do. We had already had a chat in Klintholm.

„I can't connect to the internet," the man complains, holding his smartphone in his hands. „How am I supposed to log on?"

It's true: There's no wifi here; without a working data connection to the net, there's nothing to be done. Without further ado, I give them some power by transferring my code to their pillar. At least that works.

In their many years of sailing, they had often sailed up the Swedish west coast, as they tell me, and give me lots of tips along the way. The next morning, however, their trip seems to be over for the time being: the woman had twisted her ankle when she jumped off the boat onto the jetty, and her husband now had to organise an ambulance to take her to the clinic. I admire the sprightliness with which they are still sailing in their old age. But it's not without its challenges. You're not supposed to jump off the side of the boat onto the jetty, they say, but who can always keep that in mind?

Svanen in the evening light on Utklippan

Because the wind is favourable, I pull through the 52 nautical miles to Utklippan the next day. The idea was to cross the Hanöbugten to enter the Kalmarsund directly to the north. If you have time, you could also take the route via the town of Karlskrona, which I took on the way back. However, this route would have been 15 nautical miles further, and as I am on „feeder voyage", it should be quick going. Uklippan is a special island: Already from a distance you can recognize the beacon, which stands on one of the two skerries. You enter the original, square harbour basin through a narrow entrance and then moor alongside. I catch the southeastern corner of the basin, but you can't get away from it without a dinghy, as it is surrounded by water. A colony of seagulls follows my mooring manoeuvre under protest. Here, about 15 kilometres from the Swedish mainland, it's an excellent place to spend the night, surrounded by the sound of the waves.

The Utklippan lighthouse

In Kalmar, which I reach the next day, I experience the one hundred percent contrast. After a journey of another 50 nautical miles, this time with the jib out because the wind was blowing exactly from astern, I arrived in the harbour of the town on the Kalmar Sound. Why I squeeze myself into the furthest corner, I can no longer say exactly. I moor between huge motorboat yachts, whose owners kindly help to moor them. Around me, they sit on their terraces - there's no other way to describe the yachts' spacious decks - and drink champagne from ice buckets. And they discovered that „Svanen" has Hamburg as its home port. Hamburg, Reeperbahn, Herbertstraße, the Swedish skippers rave, listing all the clichés they can think of. They seem to have been there before, they know it too well for that, I think. But it's nice that Hamburg has such a permissive reputation.

„You don't mind, Mr. Herbertstraße, if it gets a little louder, you're used to that in Hamburg," says the Swede from across the street in English, „we're having a party tonight." Well, who wants to say that it bothers him, especially if you have voluntarily squeezed in between the motorboats? I ask how loud it might get. „We'll show that in a minute," he replies. Then I get the proof: motor yacht number one (very big) is competing with motor yacht number two (not quite as big, but also stately) for the loudest sound system. And what then follows, I had never experienced in a harbour before: The basses were so deep that the glasses on board clink and the ship's side of „Svanen" shakes. The harbour master doesn't seem to mind, on the contrary, she is happy about the „action" and puts on a permanent grin. Certainly, there are many boring harbours, but this one? Hours later I capitulate and retreat to the nearest inn, while the harbour gets even louder. While I'm lying in the comfortable feather bed wondering if it wouldn't have been fun to join the party, the next moment I'm already asleep. The longer trips leave their mark.

2 THE GATEWAY TO ARCHIPELAGO SAILING

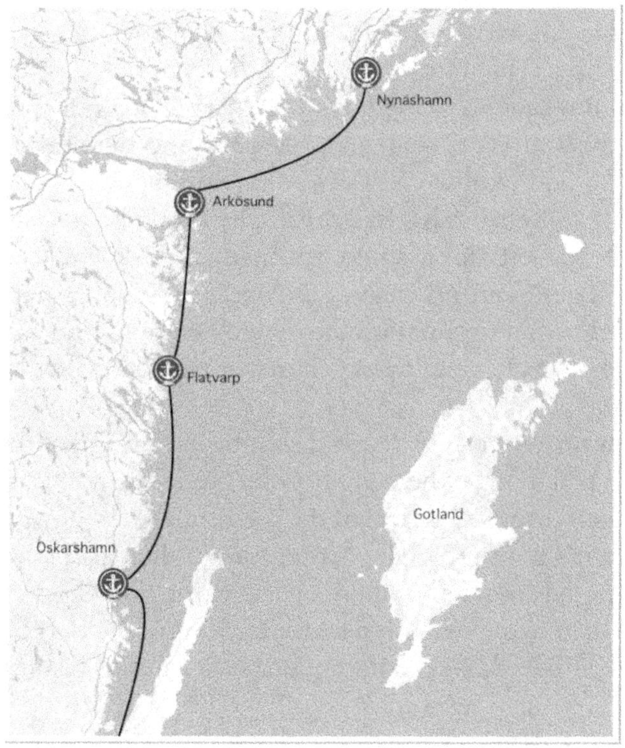

Not every town on the Swedish Baltic coast can inspire. The "picture book Sweden" is not found in all places, although in many. Before I reach the archipelago world near Västervik, I stop off in Oskarshamn on the way north from Kalmar, exactly 41.6 nautical miles away.

The entrance to Oskarshamn leads past industrial plants, a giant scrap heap until I can head for the guest harbour in the centre. First, I aim for a stern buoy, but then I go alongside the large jetty - there is hardly a boat in the harbour. A young sailor from Denmark willingly takes the lines. He and his friend are sailing a "Spaekhugger", a ship with a pointed bow and stern. The red hull and the roof structure in red-black are reminiscent of a ladybird.

"We are crisscrossing the Baltic Sea. Our boat sails quite well," he says. That means they started in Aarhus, sailed through the Little Belt, across to the Polish coast and then north again. Downright confusing, such a zigzag course. Where do they want to go? "We don't know yet. Let's see where the wind takes us," replies the sailor from his Ladybird. The funny boat is still moored at the jetty for a while, but then, as darkness sets in, the "Spaekhugger" abruptly leaves the harbour. I would have liked to ask them what destination they were heading for that night. Or do they simply want to save harbour dues? Maybe they don't know yet.

Now I turn to the city instead: A long promenade lines the harbour. At the edge, there are dozens of mobile homes. One has placed itself directly in front of the toilet house. It may be convenient, but it's not pretty. The curtains are pulled aside, a camper looks curiously, who goes there on the toilet. Somehow these vehicles irritate me when I meet them. Behind the harbour lie the shopping streets of Oskarshamn. But nice cafés or restaurants are missing. An Asian restaurant is followed by a poorly frequented pizzeria and a Turkish restaurant. I enter the latter and promptly

I am given a lesson: The kebab is served cold. I cannot understand the enthusiastic description of the city in the coastal handbook. Even the pretty Stora Torget, the main square, may not
change that: Somehow, the atmosphere reminds me of a cold day
in autumn in the fishing port in Bremerhaven.

Svanen in the port of Oskarhsman

The temperature also matches the mood: it drops to ten
degrees in the evening. Meanwhile, the ferry from Gotland
moors at the harbour, an impressive large, modern ship that also
makes a lot of noise and causes the boats to dance in the swell.

Planning the next leg is not easy. The coastal handbook lists
only a few ports for the following stretch to the north. But on the
nautical chart, I identify the small fishing port of Flatvarp at a
distance of 51 nautical miles. That's the one, even if it takes me at
least nine hours to get there. Behind the harbour exit, I set course

north. The route takes me a little way along the open Baltic Sea and past the Oskarshamn nuclear power station, one of Sweden's three active reactors.

Then "Svanen" enters the archipelago fairway between the islands of Ekö and Ängo. These islands stand between the open sea and the archipelago like the gateway to another world. The wind blows with ten to 15 knots quite well. The mainsail and the jib are standing correctly. At first, I find it scary to sail between the narrow islands. There is a wall of rocks to starboard and only a few metres further a tiny forest to port. But soon, the fairway, which leads directly north, widens a bit. The plotter shows me a clear path through this island jungle. The route I marked shines as a yellow line on the chart. And suddenly, it's fun to sail through the archipelago like this, much more fun than I had thought. On the Swedish west coast, the routes through the islands were always much busier than here. Maybe only every two hours a boat comes towards me. I leave Västervik on the port side. There is nothing to indicate that there is a small town behind the junction in the fairway.

INFO: PLANNING A TRIP

Depending on which destination you want to head for, proper cruise planning is a prerequisite. Of course, you can let yourself drift and see where you get to the next day - that can also provide wonderful sailing days. But if you have a destination in mind, you should do rough planning before the start and detailed daily planning during the trip. Where do you want to go? Do you want to sail from Lübeck to Copenhagen, which is not difficult? Do you want to go to Helgoland on the North Sea (then you can include the tidal current in your calculations, which pushes or slows, depending on where you come from)? A rule of thumb is to plan one-third of the total time to reach your destination and two thirds for the return journey. This way, you have enough reserves. We have sailed well with this on almost all trips. The daily stages are essential, as they can better respond to the current weather conditions than if you plan far in advance: A tour of 20 nautical miles is already sufficient for beginners, and even with a lot of wind and rain, this can be more than enough. If you want to make progress and the weather plays along, it can also be 40 or 60 nautical miles. Our first trip to Gothenburg, for example, was divided up like this: First four days with 40 nautical miles each. There were enough alternative ports on the Danish coast. And then the jump across the Kattegat to Sweden with 80 nautical miles. That was a long sailing day, but it went smoothly. You plan these stages in advance with a "route" that you can draw in pencil on the paper sea chart or electronically on the plotter.

The route on the screen in the midday sun

If you want to sail to distant destinations, you can also sail day and night. On the coasts of Europe, however, you should always keep your position lanterns lit at night. Otherwise, the risk of collision would be too significant. We are also helped by the active (!) AIS, which transmits our position, and the radar reflector on the mast. Then sailing at night can also be very relaxing. I find beacons and position lights show important markers more clearly than during the day. Good deck lighting is helpful if you want to work on the sails. Remember: a small crew can't sail indefinitely, and if you've been at sea all night, you'll be glad of the next port of call in the morning (unless you've already gone long and left coastal waters). In the end, it depends on the weather: if it's storming, a 60 nautical mile trip during the day is already a challenge.

Mr Moose says: *I'm not much of a planner, even though I know my territory well. And when I change my region, I have to get to know the new one very well. But navigation at sea is straightforward for me: I swim there if I see an exciting island.*

"Svanen" glides silently north. The water between the islands is almost without waves. Hour after hour passes while I operate the tiller, regularly apply sunscreen, listen to music and, on top of that, simply head north. It's like a rush that shouldn't end at all. And I know: from now on, it's almost always protected by archipelagos all the way to Stockholm. When Flatvarp is not far away anymore, I take down the sails and start the engine. I have to charge the batteries a bit. After all, I don't expect any electricity in the fishing harbour. And the diesel should give back to the batteries what the navigation has consumed during the day. I first see the port through a gap between two tree-covered islands, but it's too shallow to pass through. Then it goes around the more northerly skerry in a swing alongside the quay.

Here I am greeted by a friendly Finn who is moored with his boat in Flatvarp and moors "Svanen" perfectly. "I am Finnish," he points out in English, "even though I have a Swedish flag on the stern. I am Finnish, and we always help other sailors." I'm glad to hear that, of course. Unfortunately, I don't see much more of him; he's sitting below deck watching soccer on his laptop. Flatvarp seems to be pretty but also a bit enchanted. In the 1950s, the Swedish government had a fishing port built here in the middle of an uninhabited archipelago, from which trucks brought the goods inland. There are still a handful of fishing boats here, but otherwise, nothing at all. The harbour never developed much. The road gets lost in the forest. I have to think of none other than the "Klabautermann". The reason: During the day, I listened to many sailor shanties by the German artist Achim Reichel in the cockpit. I quote from the song of the same name: "Suddenly a crash, open the hatch. Horror paralyzes all like a man! Dripping with wetness, in ghostly pallor, in the room stands the Klabautermann!" And here I am in the dark, a dense forest all around and a cold night.

INFO: THE KLABAUTERMANN

I think that every recreational skipper travelling through the Baltic sea should know about some nautical folklore. And anyone who makes fun of the Klabautermann, or dismisses him as superstition, could be in for a nasty surprise. That's why I would like to explain the meaning of this legendary figure, which was already mentioned in the 13th century: The Klabautermann is a water goblin who traditionally helps sailors in the Baltic Sea and the North Sea with their work. He is considered to be a cheerful creature with musical talent. He is also said to help sailors who have been washed overboard. However, there is also the account according to which the Klabautermann is by no means so friendly. He should be better deterred by a chicken. The name comes from the Low German word "klabastern," which means to make a racket. Those who have tried to draw him depict him as a sailor with a whistle and a cap. But besides his good qualities, he can also mean a bad omen: It is said that the Klabautermann never shows himself. When a ship is about to sink, all crew members see him on deck. That fits it: When the boat has then sunk, no one can report on the Klabautermann either.

A beacon in the archipelago of Flatvarp

But the sun and the fresh wind from the south during the following day drive all thoughts of the Klabautermann away. I glide again through the beautiful archipelago with the breeze of five to six Beaufort. Sometimes it gets rough: You come out of the lee of an archipelago, and a gust hits and pushes the boat onto its side. And then you sail behind the next island. Suddenly, the wind pressure stops again. Arkösund is a fine little place with a history as a bathing resort for the neighbouring Norrköping. One notices that the region is getting closer to Stockholm. Magnificent villas perch on the hills around the guest harbour. And again, I moor "Svanen" with an elegant swing alongside the jetty.

The harbour fees are paid here via the Swedish system "Swoosh", which is not accessible to foreigners, or by bank transfer. This even works. Ship name and data are sent to the harbour master via SMS, the codes come back immediately.

My gaze falls on an elaborate ship washing machine with large brushes. I have seen something like this before in Bremerhaven, but here it is in operation and is just cleaning a motorboat from below. My jetty neighbours, who had overtaken me with their 11-metre Wasa yacht just before Arkösund and yet moored after me because they were still chugging along the harbour basins a bit, enlighten me. "Antifouling containing copper is no longer allowed in Sweden. This also applies to foreign boats that want to stay during the winter here. That's why these machines are popular for keeping the hull clean during the season," they tell me. The machine rattles and the rollers brush along the hull like an upside-down car wash.

My two neighbours on the jetty speak the purest Oxford English, and the cashier in the nearby supermarket sounds as if she's straight out of a BBC series.

"Isn't that lovely," she whispers as I hold out my German credit card. Less "lovely", however, is the internet connection of this sailing port: The WLAN network barely reaches the ship, and the LTE mobile phone network has dropouts. A video conference, which I conduct the next day from onboard, is repeatedly interrupted by dropouts. Even though I can show my interlocutors where I'm talking to them from with a pan of the video camera out of the cabin window - the affair gets a bit tiring. But afterwards, I have the afternoon off. And so, after work, the landlord personally welcomes me to the "Arkö Krog" and presents his menu selection to me in German. As one could call it, refined home cooking is delicious and not expensive. In addition, he serves enormous portions. The restaurant is a hit.

The next day I want to finish the feeder trip: With 44 nautical miles, Nynäshamn is within reach, the port is easily accessible by suburban train from Stockholm. But the last part has to be fought for. To save nautical miles, I choose the route outside the archipelago. And because the weather forecast agrees in almost all models that the wind will increase, I sail off now. No sooner do I leave the archipelago cover than decent waves and strong gusts are waiting for "Svanen". Nobody seems to be out here, on this stretch of the coast off Oxelösund, where it's blowing at six Beaufort. This becomes exhausting as the wave hits the boat diagonally from astern. This leads to an unpleasant rolling. After all, "Svanen" is as fast as an arrow and races towards Nynäshamn at over six knots. With her banking, "Svanen" must have looked somewhat dramatic. First, a cruiser from the Swedish coast guard comes by. The crew seems curious about what a sailor is doing out here. With a friendly wave, they say goodbye. Then the supply ship of a wind farm detours from its course and goes alongside in the choppy sea. A worried captain waves from his wheelhouse, and I wave back cheerfully. He calmly returns to his old course.

But what is this, I think. Just a moment ago, I was watching a row of rocks rising out of the sea, then my eyes fell on the tablet with the navigation, and now it's dark. The tablet plotter has gone bye-bye. Without a plotter, with only the paper sea chart, I don't want to sail here. I have to activate the replacement device in the cabin, an older Garmin plotter, which at least shows me the position on the chart and the next archipelago. In addition, it rolls and some wave that hits the ship sprays the cockpit wet. For the first time, it occurs to me that the "Svanen", which is just under nine metres long, might not have enough reserves for this weather. And neither does her skipper. Although I hardly ever get seasick, I now feel nauseous after hours of rocking.

Öja is the name of the island I'm heading for. North of it, there is a passage at the Äspsk skerry, which leads back into the sheltered sea. Up and down, the ship tilts, simultaneously to port and starboard. A few more times, then it is done, "Svanen" crosses the passage. Behind the island, it is still blowing, but the water is smooth mainly again so that I can set a relaxed last hour before I reach Nynäshamn. As a sailor's saying goes, "It's not the wind the sailor fears, but the wave." That applies to this trip.

The picturesque harbour of Arkösund

The next day I first install the old plotter permanently. Sceptically I look at the tablet on the bulkhead, which runs the navigation software "Open CPN". The power plug is not securely seated in its socket. Unnoticed, the device had switched to the battery, and when it was empty, it went off. I'm taking it upon myself: If the main plotter fails, a replacement unit must be available in a few seconds, which is an essential requirement in these archipelagos.

Nynäshamn has a beautiful, vast sailing harbour and a less charming town centre. If you walk up Centralgatan and then past the pretty Nynäshamn Kirka, visible from afar, you'll come to the centre. Behind the Kulturhuset, a concrete building equal to the "Palast der Republik" in Berlin, the concrete facades of numerous high-rise buildings rise. Unfortunately, there are not many shops in the centre. It is nicer down at the harbour, where there is a row of shops with lovely little stalls on the waterfront offering ice cream and handicrafts. There are also many bars and restaurants there, visited by guests, who all do not wear a mask.

As I make myself comfortable in the cockpit, a Vindö 50 named "Alysa" slowly passes the stern. This type of boat is the father of the Vindö 32, a little longer, a little wider, and a few years older. She was the godfather of our ship.

"We are on our way to Hamburg," the skipper calls out to me as she passes "Svanen". "We are moving from Helsinki to Hamburg and transferring our ship." Great, I reply to her. I've done ship crossings before, for example, from Berlin to Bremen. But straight from Helsinki? I'm impressed.

Opposite, a Polish yacht from Gdansk is moored at the jetty. While I watch "Alysa", the skipper unpacks his guitar. A cluster of people forms at the stern of his ship while he sings Polish songs. I listen for a bit, not understanding anything, of course, until, like a Polish cliché, he starts singing drinking songs. "Pijemy wódke i gin, wódke i ginî - it's not hard to guess what that means, and a few minutes later, they're toasting each other. There's a friendly, international atmosphere in the harbour here.

When I then see the big ferry to Poland, which just arrived in Nynäshamn, I wonder whether it would not also be an alternative for the return trip. One would only have to get from Gdansk to Hamburg because now I have to go back to Germany for two weeks.

A nice wind takes me through the archipelago

By the way, Nynäshamn harbour offers a very cheap rate by Scandinavian standards with a ten euro berthing fee per day when no one is on board. The ferry to Poland is fully booked, and I decide on the "classic" route: a suburban train to Stockholm and the "Snabbtåg", the Swedish high-speed train, in about four hours to Gothenburg. From there, the Stena Line ferry takes me back to Germany. A flight would have been even more straightforward, but the trip via Gothenburg promised to be more interesting.

Travelling by the train called X2000 is also fun because the interior is a nice mix of Scandinavian design in the style of the eighties. The wide, comfortable upholstered chairs are more reminiscent of a retro living room than a fast train, unlike an ICE in Germany. But the "Snabbtåg" is also running a hefty delay of one hour. So be it, because a little later this Sunday evening, I am sitting in the bar of the ferry that leaves Gothenburg and its river Göta Alv under the big Älsborgbron. There is hardly anyone on board here. The tables are almost all empty. "Yes, it's really not very busy. It's just Corona summer. Not many people take the ferry," shrugs the waitress.

I think back to when we've sailed through this part of Sweden. We were here twice before, in Gothenburg. Outside, the wind picks up, sweeping between the western Swedish archipelago and churning up the water. The islands look rougher beyond the window than on the Swedish east coast, partly because they are less forested. At this moment, for once, I'm quite happy to be on a large ferry. It only vibrates a little and is barely pushed on its side by the wind - not like a sailboat.

3 FINALLY IN THE ARCHIPELAGO

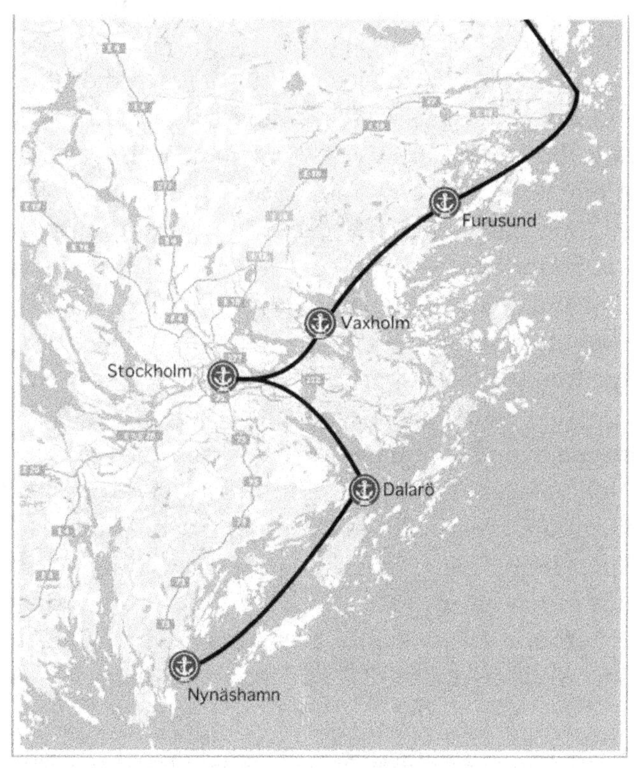

nyone studying a nautical chart of the Stockholm archipelago for the first time could quickly feel overwhelmed. There are hundreds of islands, many small passages, and routes too shallow for a keelboat and those requiring significant detours around individual islands. Stockholm is located on many islands and not on the banks of a river, like Hamburg or Bremen. Our coastal handbook does not necessarily contribute to clarity either. It lists complicatedly formulated routes that it numbers from "1" to "6b". But the confusion doesn't have to be there at all. As there are three simple ways to get to Stockholm. Those from the south can first take the way through the back door. This would be the lock at Södertälje that leads into the inland lake Mälaren that borders at the east to Stockholm.

Furthermore, there is the possibility to reach the city from the southwest. This route passes the sailing village of Saltsjöbaden. And those who come from the north will take the route via Vaxholm that is also used by the ferries from Finland. For us, it is clear, we go via Saltsjöbaden because the entrance into the Mälaren at Södertälje is already behind us. After all, I had moored "Svanen" in Nynäshamn.

On a beautiful Sunday in July, we land, coming from Hamburg, at the airport in Stockholm-Arlanda. Now the actual part of our trip can begin. The fast airport shuttle and the less fast suburban train bring us to the harbour. It is hard to believe that we only left Hamburg in the morning to be already on board in the afternoon. Despite all discussions: Such a flight is practical and inexpensive.

But it is much nicer to see "Svanen" well-protected at the jetty. The harbour masters of Nynäshamn have taken good care of the boat. All lines are tight. In addition, a modern battery is waiting for us: we sent the so-called LifePo4 power storage unit by post to avoid all debates about airline luggage. It has been delivered to a kiosk in Nynäshamn as a mail depot. Its purpose is to supply power to the freezer to avoid a drain on the boat's central battery bank.

With a small stretch from Nynäshamn to Dalarö, about 21 nautical miles, we start the trip through the archipelago. Among several destinations, this seemed to be the most attractive harbour. When the peninsula appears in the afternoon, we are not disappointed: we see picture book cottages built on the slopes of an archipelago and a lovely harbour.

A café in Dalarö

The Swede who has moored next to us in Dalarö dreams of "trips to the big wide world", as he tells us from his cockpit. I reassure him: "You have one of the most attractive sailing areas on your doorstep." But he wants to go further away and knows almost every Youtube channel of sailors on their way to faraway destinations. And he also plans financially: In the evening he sets off, the mooring fees in Dalarö, which are a proud 36 euros per night, are too high for him. By the way, there is a cafe in the harbour of Dalarö. One pays approximately 18 euros for a home-made sausage there. The archipelago is an expensive place.

After dark, music resounds over the harbour again. I know immediately who I'm dealing with. "Pijemy wódke i gin, wódke i ginî", sings the Polish skipper, who had already made music in Nynäshamn two weeks ago. And again, there is a toast on his ship. But the Swedes in Dalarö are less tolerant: Another sailor asks him to stop the "disturbance of the peace" immediately. It is already almost midnight. A look into the sky cannot confirm this: It is still quite bright. It is actually a pity that it is suddenly quiet in the harbour because I found the Poles and their guitar quite atmospheric.

INFO: THE NAVIGATION

"Svanen" proves with her large chart table and the "cutlery", which is always ready at hand on the bulkhead, that she was laid on keel in the time of paper charts. Here you can still plan your routes precisely with a pencil, ruler and compass - something every skipper must be able to do. But of course, today, electronic navigation is standard. In the US, for example, paper nautical charts are no longer issued, as it is believed that every boater has electronic navigation.

In principle, you have three options, all of which we have tried: Buy a chart plotter and the appropriate charts for their unit. You can usually just connect the plotter to a 12-volt battery on board and, if you like, additionally connect it to the instru-ments. Pros: a relatively simple operation, waterproof and read-able even in sunlight in the cockpit. Cons: This is the most expensive solution, and it is installed stationary on board.

Then you can resort to an "app" solution, such as "Boating

HD" from Navionics. Smartphones or tablets almost always have built-in GPS these days. Advantages: A tablet can be used anywhere on board and at home. It is cheaper than a chart plotter and maps. Disadvantages: Tablets are often not waterproof, and their screens are rarely bright enough (1200 candela and up) to be read in the cockpit in the sun. And finally, the third solution is a do-it-yourself chart plotter. For this, you take a small PC with Windows or Linux. Also the hobby computer "Raspberry Pi" has what it takes. You couple it with a screen as bright as possible, which you mount in the cockpit. As software, the open-source solution "Open CPN" offers many functions. This can be equipped cheaply with current nautical charts from the provider "o-charts", which are available for almost all European cruising areas. Advantages: mostly cheaper than a plotter and a flexible system. Disadvantages: Quite a bit of fiddling, a PC is more complex than a plotter. You need additional devices if you want to integrate your instruments or even the autopilot. Which solution has prevailed on board? After many experiments with Open CPN and onboard PCs, we had a waterproof and safe chart plotter.

Mr. Moose says: Don't make it too complicated for yourself. After all, your sailing also requires a lot of attention. Pick a method, get the charts, and you can plan. It's best to do this before you set sail. Luckily I am a moose.

. . .

The fairway becomes narrower and narrower the next day when we approach Stockholm between Saltsjöbaden and the village of Boo, which flows into the main fairway north of Kungshamn. What is especially noticeable here is the many Swedish motorboats on the way in the archipelago. They come from starboard and port and make huge stern waves that sway many sailboats. They hum loudly and obviously happily cruise at 20 knots and more. I don't envy them, but I'm sure that this is an example of how the stereotype of the climate-conscious Swede, which many Germans want to romanticise, doesn't apply on the water. No, they are annoying, the many motorboats, but as a guest, you have to accept that, of course. I don't begrudge them the fun of driving, if only - slosh - my coffee hadn't spilt out of my cup when we passed another wake.

A speed limit in the narrow fairway then makes everyone equal again. Sailors and motorboat drivers alike have to squeeze through the narrow waterway a little later. The small channel even passes a cemetery. The entrance to Stockholm over the central canal is almost majestic: one passes motorboats and sailors on the way into the city and dozens of archipelago steamers and other excursion boats. In the distance, the famous town hall tower glitters in the sun. We sail around the island of Djurgården and pass the Gröna Lund amusement park, whose roller coasters reach almost to the top of our mast. In Wasahamnen harbour, I have booked a couple of nights, again in style with the app, the way they do it in Sweden these days.

I get the hook for the stern buoy out of "Svanen's" locker. So far, we have managed without it. But I can only recommend such a hook. One swing, the clamp locks in place, the line is firmly attached to the buoy. I like this uncomplicated system.

Why Wasahamnen? The advantage is obvious: it is located in the centre of Stockholm. Those entering the capital from Lake Mälaren can, of course, also moor in Västerbrohamnen, which is still in front of a lock. But otherwise, there is little competition to Wasahamnen. Behind the famous Wasa-museum, one gets via the Djurgårdsvägen to the beautiful avenue Strandvägen. This leads to the place Nybroviken, where the archipelago steamers moor. Of course, you can also rent one of the many e-scooters. They are the same providers as in Hamburg or Berlin, and the app works here too. But watch out: The Stockholmers drive downright breakneck with the small electric scooters.

What is the best way to explore Stockholm? There are numerous travel guides about this. We do it this way the next day: We take the ferry to the pier Stockholm Slussen Kajen, we walk through the oldtown, past the castle and then once through the modern centre. The city centre of Stockholm has been built up with a lot of concrete, the urge to the architectural modernity of the sixties is very conspicuous. But in between there are also a lot of lovely shops, restaurants and cafés. Especially in the centre, it is crowded, and again it is noticeable that nobody keeps a distance in Corona times, and hardly anybody wears a mask.

The only supermarket seems to be in the subway station. I have to literally "fight" for the food through the queues. Unfortunately, there is one rain shower after the other, and the air is quite humid. But just then, it is wonderful to live in the middle of the city on the water, on our sailboat. This is also the opinion of our sailing neighbour from Berlin. He has taken a sabbatical over two summer seasons - a rather clever construction that he has arranged with his employer, I think. His boat is to remain in Sweden over the winter so that the couple can continue sailing next year.

Grönalund amusement park, Wasahamn behind it

Stockholm offers so much variety. We even stroll to Grönalund the following evening. The temptation to ride a round of roller coasters is great. In the end, only the hunger keeps us away from it, as we are in front of a nice restaurant, we leave the amusement park on the left.

We still stay in the Stockholm area and head for Vaxholm, only about 10.5 nautical miles away. We head northeast through the busy main fairway, which many ferries cross. Vaxholm has a really nice harbour. It seems like an actual sailing suburb. There is a good ship's chandler where we buy new fenders, as the old ones are already quite battered. Further, a nearby supermarket includes "Systembolaget", the state-licensed alcohol shops where you have to buy stronger beer, wine, and other alcoholic beverages. And there is a nice bathing spot with a café a few hundred meters south of the harbour, where a jump into the clear water of the archipelago follows.

I'm just putting away our new supplies in the boat when I hear excited voices. An old Swede is heading for the berth next to ours with his motorboat. Vaxholm harbour has "mooring lines", which are lines coming from the jetty to the bottom where they are anchored. There are no stern poles, no buoys, but lines that you pick up at the front and then attach to the stern. And just at this moment, the motorboat's propeller gets caught in one of these lines. No forward, no back. It is stuck diagonally to the berth and seems quite helpless. A big motor yacht had brought him out of the concept, which moored quite rapidly opposite.

What to do in such a case? Either jump into the water yourself or, as the harbour master advises, call a diver. He seemed to be already standing by. In any case, he is there in a few minutes with his professional equipment. The diver disappears into the harbour basin with an oxygen tank and unties the mooring line. He doesn't cut anything but leaves the line undamaged as a professional. The Swedish skipper is finally able to moor the boat.

These days belong to the Stockholm archipelago. The next day we travel northeast in the main fairway. Many ferries pass us on their way from the capital to the Åland Islands and Finland. In front of the island "Yxlan", a speedboat of the coast guard approaches us. At precisely the same speed, the skipper sails parallel to us, and one of the officers cross-examines us: where we come from, what we want, where we entered? I am astonished. I have already crossed the Swedish border four weeks ago near Ystad. Of course, he also wants to know if we have tobacco or alcohol on board. I can reassure the policeman: Cigarettes are more expensive in Germany than in Sweden, which is why it wouldn't be worth taking any with us. He casts a somewhat uncertain glance at his superior as if to say: What do we do now? With a wave of his hand, he tells him that he can let "Svanen" go. The skipper accelerates, and the coast guard disappears again. Apparently, they check many ships here because we see them checking another yacht a little later. In such moments with somewhat grim police officers, I am glad to be in Sweden, or rather in the European Union country.

Fully occupied: Svanen is right in the centre

The country is also known for the books by Astrid Lindgren. And we moor in Furusund, a harbour on the island where Astrid Lindgren had a cottage. August Strindberg also spent several summer holidays here and included motifs from the island in his collection of novellas "Fagervik and Skamsund". Is it necessary to mention that Furusund is still a beautiful, relaxed little place? The fairway is relatively narrow here, and the big ferries still pass the pretty place with its colourful tiny houses brightly lit in the evening. Finally, the sauna is open. In Nynäshamn, for example, there was also a nice harbour sauna, but it was closed with a big seal of the municipality with reference to the Corona pandemic. But in Furusund the oven crackles away at 95 degrees in the wooden cabin. With the rainy weather outside, it's just the right change.

In the evening, I sit in front of our autopilot in the glow of the cabin lighting. The device gave up the ghost in the afternoon, but I can't find any fault. Such an autopilot will be essential for the long distances ahead of us on the way north. But the Raymarine is on strike. So I get out the spare unit, an older model. It seems to still be running. I plug it in and get it ready.

The next day, "Svanen" sails in serpentine lines, which must have led to the confusion of some other sailors who carefully keep their distance from our ship. The practical test shows that the replacement autopilot does not seem to be up to the task. It constantly over-steers, after which I have to correct it by hand. It looks like this: "Yes, the course is right, 90 degrees," I say with a glance at the compass. "Oh, the bow is drifting a little to port. No, way too much." I have to switch the autopilot to "standby", correct the course by hand, and set it back to "auto". No, that's not going to work with the autopilot. I disengage the apparatus as the trip continues north. An unsolved problem. But nothing can help me get over this immediate disappointment like a stop for a swim in the archipelago. The clouds have cleared, and it gets really hot in the sun. If we leave the technical problems aside, at least the weather omens are not bad for the trip north.

4 THE ROUTE TO THE HIGH COAST

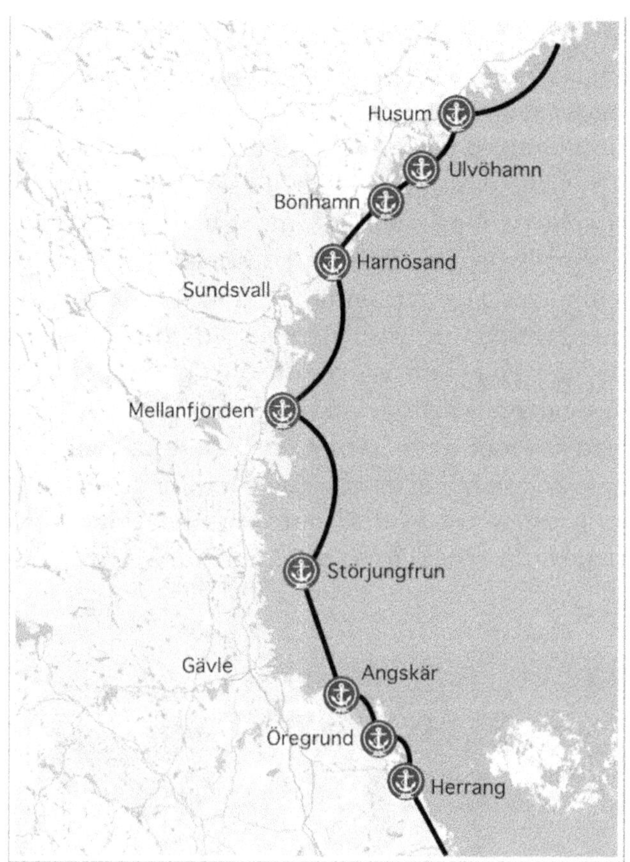

We have called many ports north of Stockholm on our round trip around the Bothnian Sea. One gets into that sea either along the coast to the north or through the Vaddö channel that directly connects to the archipelago. On a length of five nautical miles, the waterway was built that runs between two archipelago islands. Only in front of two bascule bridges, the sailor has to wait with his high mast. Before that, one can sail along the narrow blue band between meadows and pastures as if one would sail inland. Behind the small place Hammarby, the fairway gets a little wider again, even though there are still some 10 nautical miles until the archipelago waters north of Stockholm are reached. On the way, a bridge with a fixed passage height of 17 metres has to be passed. Thus, the passage is denied to sailing yachts with higher masts. After 40 nautical miles, we moor in the harbour of Herrang. Shortly before, our actual destination, the port of Grisslehamn, was a disappointment: Stones lay right up to the guest berths, which were also all occupied, in addition, there were loads of mobile homes everywhere on the shore. Not a nice place. Herrang, on the other hand, is probably only visited by locals. I had not found the harbour in any guide, only on the sea chart. There are plenty of empty guest moorings right in front of the harbour restaurant. With 20 euros the mooring fee is cheap, and also the restaurant is to be recommended. An insider tip, I would say.

Heading north through the Vaddö Canal

In the small town of Öregrund, we make a shopping stop the next day. The jetties reach almost to the door of the local ICA supermarket. But the places close to the supermarket are all reserved for locals. A little nervous, we moor our yacht close to the grocery store. I hurry up, race to the store, quickly throw everything into a shopping cart that seems worthwhile, especially lots of drinks, as it's getting quite hot outside again. Quickly paid and packed all the goods in bags and out to the ship. All went well. No one has "upset" the boat. We can calmly depart again.

Then we pass the second nuclear power plant to Oskarshamn, Forsmark. The colossal plant has its own approach. And it is only shortly before the power station harbour that the archipelago fairway, which we want to follow, turns to the north. Forsmark can produce 3000 megawatts of electricity, and Sweden still gets half of its electricity from nuclear energy. Therefore, the electricity prices are one-third of the fees in the middle of Europe. However, it is reassuring when the plant disappears from view after a few nautical miles.

Behind the peninsula Angskär, we turn into a small fjord to reach the harbour of the same name. Clear water washes around the pier where we moor "Svanen". Only four other guest boats have stopped here, among them a friendly Swiss. He has already sailed a long distance in the Bothnian Sea and is now already on his way south again. The small facility is not listed in any sailing guide, but it is worth visiting. It is located in the middle of the nature reserve.

The water simply teases you to unfold the swim ladder. With a "splash", the stainless steel descends into the clear water. As I climb in, I notice: That's cold. Much colder than in the archipelago. And yet, it's the middle of July. But the thermometer shows me a little later that the Bothnian Sea has only 15 degrees Celsius here. 216 nautical miles lie in the wake since the start of the actual stage in Nynäshamn. It were 33 nautical miles to Angskär.

INFO: SLEEP WELL ON BOARD

The importance of a good night's sleep should not be underesti-
mated when cruising. Sailing unrested can be not only very
uncomfortable but also risky. So what do you need? Two factors
are significant: the correct sizing of the berths and the underlay.
If you want as large a berth as possible, you should be aware that
it promises plenty of comfort in port but that at sea, you'll need
something to brace against - otherwise, you'll be rocked back and
forth by the waves. A narrow, secured berth for underway and a
large one for the night in port or at anchor would be ideal.

Berth size does not necessarily depend on the size of the ship,
as we found out for ourselves. We had a spacious forward berth
on our small cruiser, the 6.20 metre long Kelt. However, on our
"Jaguar 25", it was so small that two adults could not really sleep
there. We converted the saloon for this, setting up two folding
mattresses that went the entire width of the ship. This was a
massive two by two-metre berth. When the bed was folded out,
there was not much room left in the boat. The cabin was more or
less just one big bed. But as soon as you are on a vessel of nine
metres or more in length, you will have enough space in the
saloon in addition to the forward berth (the so-called V-berth).
On "Svanen", we can use the V-berth in the harbour and fold out
a berth in the saloon at sea.

The pad should be such that you can sleep more or less as
you would at home. This is a matter of personal preference. But
rarely are the ship's pads alone sufficient as a mattress. We put
isomats on the wood of the forward berth, a fabric about 1.5 cm
high on top of that, and the pads on top of that. This gives a stiff
but springy base over which air can also get to the cushions
below. I had cut a flat slatted frame for the bunk on the small
cruiser, which worked perfectly. The longer a cruise gets, the

greater your sleeping requirements will be. After a few weeks, even a sufficient pad at the beginning will become very hard. By the way, it does not necessarily have to be special mattresses for ships, which are offered quite expensively. A rigid foam mattress can also be cut to fit the shape of your ship's berth if you have taken exact measurements beforehand and sewn around the cover. Also: If you sail high in the north in summer, darker curtains in front of the bunk windows are a fine thing. Otherwise, you can wake up at three o'clock in the morning with the sun beating down on your bunk. Sleep is then no longer to think of.

Mr. Moose says: Ahh, sleep, an excellent topic. By the way, we moose spend most of our time eating, but after that comes sleep. We don't lie down, though, but lean against a nice tree for a nap. No, you can't try that on your ships. So get yourself a good base for rest.

The next day the coast slowly disappears on the horizon. We have now set the course exactly north, towards the island of Storjungfrun. The southern part of the Bothnian Sea is called the "Gulf of Bothnia" on our large sea chart, which we now cross from south to north. From a distance, we can see the small, thick lighthouse that stands on a hill on Storjungfrun. This islet is a highlight of the trip so far. Around the harbour, where the boats share a few stern buoys, there are tiny wooden houses, the paths are covered with wooden planks. There is also a sauna house. But you won't find electricity and water here. Instead, the harbour is decorated with flower pots, next to which the boat crews set up their barbecues in the evening. There are a lot of Finns here. For them, it is only a short jump across the "Gulf" to the Swedish side. On the 10th July, it is still very bright here at midnight.

Almost as beautiful as the island, but more extensive, is the village of Mellanfjorden, which we head for the next day. The spot lies at the end of a fjord. There, where a small river flows in, there are small wooden fisher huts on a pearl necklace at the shore. Some seem to still serve fishermen. Others have been converted into holiday apartments. A pretty café has opened next to it, run by locals on a volunteer basis. They've baked cakes for their café, which are displayed in a glass case. And the operator explains to us that she could only take cash. That's a rarity in Sweden, she explains with a laugh.

Next to "Svanen", a local is working on his boat at the mooring, which stands out because it is only 2.20 metres wide, but almost 13 metres long. He has just bought the boat and is now getting it ready for the journey.

"I want to go to Greece with this," he explains. "That's where I just came from, and it's just as hot there as it is here," he adds as he wipes the sweat from his brow. The temperature has increased in the days since we left Stockholm. The days are hot.

"Once we have stable summer weather, experience shows, it stays that way." He wants to transfer his boat to Greece pragmatically: In September, he will sail to Travemünde. There a truck will be ready to transport the vessel to Croatia. Until then, he still has a lot of work ahead of him because his cruiser is getting a bit long in the tooth.

"It's fast for that," he says. With the shape of the boat, there's no question about that. It is always a pleasure to see unusual ships that stand out from the uniformity of white GRP yachts of recent construction when visiting marinas. And this cruiser is one of them. Because I would like to charge the batteries on board, the Swede helps us out with an ultra-long cable. We are moored at a quay intended initially for fishing boats and where there is only one power socket far away.

The heat is replaced by a fresh wind the next day as we sail further north. Unfortunately, there is also some wave again, which catches the stern from behind - a direction that does not get "Svanen" so well, as I had to find out before Nynäshamn. After a few hours, however, we can enter the fjord, through which we approach the small town of Härnösand from the south. Here, the "Höga Küsten", the high coast, begins. To confirm this, shortly before Härnösand, the first skiing area appears on the starboard side. Of course, the lift frames and the green slopes with the ski runs look unreal in the summertime, especially if one sees them from the boat. But the slopes are steep.

However, the bridge keeper of Härnösand does not answer his phone, although I try all numbers I find on the net. Without the bascule bridge, we don't get into the city. But as soon as we turn the next corner, there is a yacht in front of us and the first bridge opens. We are pretty lucky. The bridge keeper is on duty, even without being reachable by phone. Härnösand is a small city that nevertheless seems to be a big city. In the northern guest harbour the traffic roars past the shore. In the park in the centre there is an open-air concert. And before that, many drunks on the promenade can hardly keep themselves on their feet.

The city centre with some empty shops is unfortunately only moderately attractive. But the city has donated a beautiful pontoon for the yachts that dock here. The brand new sanitary facilities were co-financed by the EU, as a sign announces. Actually, there would be room for several hundred boats here, but no more than a dozen have moored. Instead, the band at the Skeppet restaurant on the waterfront is rocking the hell out of it. Many open-air visitors have moved on here, and entertainment is guaranteed for the night.

With a loud ringing the following day the bridge calls for

departure. The bridge keeper is on duty again. So now it goes to the Höga coast. This coast stretches from Härnösand in the south to Örnsköldsvik, over a distance of 85 kilometres. Here the steep hills drop directly into the sea. Since 2000, this landscape has been a Unesco World Heritage Site. It is not unlike the archipelago in the south, except that the islands are much higher and steeper. For example, the island of Mjaltön, for instance, is Sweden's highest island, rising 236 metres from the water. And the land continues to increase, by about 0.8 centimetres per year. That's where we're heading now: From Härnösand behind the island Hemsön through, then to starboard into the Storfjärden, where you can have a look at a gigantic suspension bridge. It crosses the fjord, which reaches far inland, as a part of the European Road 4. Behind the island of Storön, we went again a bit into the open sea, which greets us with plenty of waves. Therefore, we choose a way further north around the island of Barstaön, in order to then take a big bend at Höglosmen, which should lead us to the well-known harbour of Bönhamn. Fortunately, we manage to do this in just a few minutes before we are hit by a squall that covers everything in heavy rain and takes away our visibility.

Moored in the harbour of Störjungfrun

Bönhamn is well known, an idyllic place with carefully reno-vated fishermen's houses and a small harbour in the middle of the Höga coast. Therefore, it is also crowded this summer evening. We haven't seen so many boats in one place since Stock-holm. We find a place for "Svanen" with difficulty, which is moored in front of a jetty. With stern anchor and lines stretched to the next house, we moor. I think it holds pretty well, but a Swedish motorboat driver has a different opinion. Without asking, he starts to untie the lines and moor them again. That is too much generosity. Despite my request to just leave the ropes now, he doesn't stop and undoes knot after knot. It took a few more attempts before he let go of the boat, somewhat offended. I can't make sense of it, nor can our boat neighbours from Germany. They are sailing an "Ohlson 8:8", which measures precisely 8.80 metres. The skipper bought the boat mainly for this trip to welcome the early retirement in the Bothnian Sea with a friend. The two are enthusiastic about Sweden, but less so about Finland. There are hardly any harbours there, and they are also primitive in their equipment. Above all, they warn us against the "recommended routes" of the sea chart in Finland, the routes that lead through the archipelago. How well-founded these concerns are, we will find out later at Oulu.

"Instead of chartering, we just bought a boat," he explains. "That's when we thought we now owned a reasonably sized yacht. Then we come here and find it's the smallest boat." True: Those who sail (and don't take a motorboat) in Sweden usually have a new and large sailing yacht. You see small or even older boats here less often than in Germany or Denmark.

Is it because of the higher income of the Swedes? The prices charged by the restaurant right next to the berth seem to speak for it. Here you can get hamburgers that cost 18 euros, a new highlight in the price level. But they are locally produced and taste quite good. But I can't help thinking that Bönhamn and its restaurateurs are cashing in on the place's popularity. This does not diminish the area. But I cannot quite understand the enthusiasm that many sailors fall into when talking about the Höga coasts. Much more idyllic is the place we head for the next day.

But first, we had to get the boat loose. In addition to the lines to the land, we have deployed a stern anchor. It is now stuck in the harbour basin, and we have to loosen it with some tugging.

Worth a detour on the way is the place Ulvöhamn, which lies on the island of Norra Ulvön. Coming from the west, we enter a narrow fjord. And in it, a semicircular bay opens up with a small town with jetties where fishermen and recreational skippers are moored, with hotels and holiday homes. On the other side, it goes to the northeast out of the fjord and onto the water of the Bothnian Sea. I can only recommend this place to everybody. The "Hamnavgift", the harbour fee, is with 250 crowns in the upper range for the Bothnian Sea, but still cheaper than in the south of Sweden. And the facilities are well maintained. This beautiful place is perfect for a stop. And especially when it's windy, and the waves rock the boat, a stopover in the sheltered, quiet fjord of Ulvön is worthwhile. When a North German hears of Husum, he immediately thinks of the "grey town by the sea", as the German writer Theodor Storm called it. And, of course, Husum can be reached from the North Sea, depending on the tide. But there is also a Husum in Sweden, completely without tide, in the middle of the shore of the Gulf of Bothnia. The harbour is a lot bigger than the German "original Husum". The reason for this can be seen in the large paper factory. But the town itself is much smaller. Husum is conveniently located on our route, so we steer past the freighters moored at the quay of the paper mill. This plant dominates everything here. The mill is by far the largest employer in this area. As the construction cranes show, the gigantic industrial plant is being expanded.

The navigation is not easy, because the nautical charts do not show a guest harbour. Only the old Garmin shows the newer representatives Navionics and "Open CPN" once again how it works: The magenta-coloured symbol for a guest harbour lies behind the industrial port, hidden in a bay into which a river flows. We keep our eyes open and then find the jetty of the local sailing club, just deep enough in the land to hide the view of the industrial facilities. And it is worth the visit because it is much nicer than some tourist harbours at the Höga coasts. Only a tiny motorboat from Umeå is moored on the wooden jetty as a guest mooring alongside the local boats.

On foot, we make our way through the suburb of Husum to find a restaurant. There are two, just opposite each other. One is closed, the other serves pizza. The team of the local football club is being fed there at the moment. So that can't be all bad, I suppose. In fact, we are served giant Swedish pizza. It's not bad, and the portions are so generous that it's as if we're hard-working paper factory workers. At least hard-working sailors, that's what we are.

On the quay in the small town of Harnösand

5 UP THROUGH THE QUARK

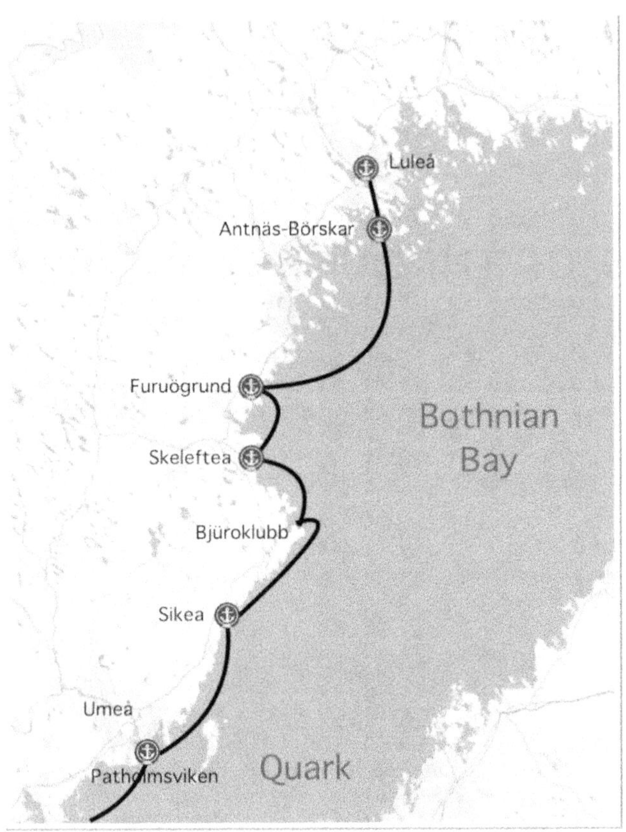

The Quark divides the southern from the northern part of the Bothnian Sea, more precisely, the Bottenhavet of Västerbotten. The region connects to Höga Kusten when coming from the south. I had always noticed the name "Quark" in the weather forecasts of the German Weather Service DWD. How can an area only be called "Quark"? The sea area we are now entering in Swedish is called "Kvarken". That sounds even scarier. The Quark is a relatively flat area where the coasts of Sweden and Finland come closer to each other. Therefore, there are a lot of skerries here again. On the Swedish side, there is the city of Umeå with approximately 83,000 inhabitants, about as big as Flensburg in Germany. We completed the trip with a very good, aft wind, which drives us quickly to the north. The only passenger ferry crosses the Bothnian Sea here, heading for Vaasa on the Finnish side. We only have to avoid it, then we can enter the harbour of Patholmsviken.

Umeå lies on the river Ume älv, but the bridges at the river's mouth are so low at 3.80 metres that sailing yachts can no longer sail to the town. But the sailing club of Patholmsviken at the mouth of the river offers everything your heart desires.

A friendly, helpful community of sailors that maintains a beautiful clubhouse, where the sanitary facilities and a sauna and a large club room are located and whose kitchen can be used. Behind the clubhouse, the world ends for the time being because there is a boat storage area on a large open space. Only then follows a settlement with single-family houses laid out in a US-American checkerboard pattern.

Who now decides to get to know the city from the harbour of the sailing club has to overcome several obstacles. First, you have to reach the bus station a few kilometres away. Then the local bus operator, who no longer accepts cash and credit cards, requires you to play the app on your smartphone, register there and have your credit card details authorized. Only then can I buy a bus ticket. This also has to be validated in the vehicle, at a barcode scanner, which the bus driver, who again speaks no English, tries to make me understand with increasing impatience. I would say: Well done, you can hardly better prevent that strangers visit the town of Umeå, if they do not arrive with their own car or by taxi.

The 35-minute bus ride along the little river is very scenic. I found the visit to Umeå interesting. It is a university town. There is a downtown with a pedestrian mall and some shopping arcades. Yes, there are a handful of restaurants and cafes there. But: Nothing stands out from the usual uniformity you find all over European cities. The inevitable H&M is followed by other chains, and also, the gastronomy seems to consist exclusively of chain stores. But the park behind the city hall, which stretches along the river as a boardwalk and has been designed in an appealing and modern way, breaks up the uniform picture a little. In the afternoon, the bus leaves the city again and returns to the suburb with its friendly sailing harbour.

Let's travel north through the Quark sea area: There you pass a group of islands, to which the archipelagos Holmöarna, Ängesön and Grundviken belong. They are all located in a nature reserve. Byviken offers a small harbour with a bathing beach and grocery store and a small maritime museum.

In these archipelagos, Mr Moose might start to appear, I think. After all, the question of the swimming moose is still on my mind. But no matter how closely I look at the water and the small islands, I can't spot Mr Moose here yet. He is not so common in the south and centre of Sweden. I will have to wait a little longer until we have left the busy archipelago areas.

We head for Sikeå, the harbour of a former shipyard where the local yacht club runs a guest harbour. On the way, we have wind from the east and sound waves. "Svanen" lays heavily on her side but holds her course well. Soon, the spook is over. As we approach the wide entrance to the bay, the water is almost smooth, even though the wind is still blowing hard. Next to us, a big wooden yacht moors. Behind the wheelhouse windows sits a big cat, which follows the mooring manoeuvre attentively. The clubhouse of the harbour is housed in a small wooden house. Here you pay the harbour dues in cash into a cash box. You can also use the beautiful sauna for a few crowns extra, which has a window overlooking the nearby forest. Information boards show the history of the place. Actually, it's hard to imagine there was once a large harbour where two- and three-masters were built 80 years ago. Not much more than the quay is left of it.

The wind has increased the next day. The sailors at the quay in Sikeå agree that they do not want to sail today. But we decide to give it a try after all. When the wind gauge shows 16 knots, that leaves enough reserves for our heavy long keeler. And outside, it works out well: with strong gusts, we continue up the coast until we reach a peninsula, where the coastline gives way to the west again.

There lies the tiny harbour of Bjüroklubb. Actually, a beautiful place, situated at the tip of a headland with a hill on which a lighthouse stands. But here we have no chance: A gigantic motor yacht blocks several berths of the small pilot harbour. Behind it, stern lines are stretched criss-cross across the harbour basin, where every square metre of water seems to be occupied by boats. Even if we had absolutely had to: There's no way to moor here. I have to steer backwards out of the harbour, but in doing so the stern bangs against the harbour wall at the entrance. A loud crack can be heard, the shaft of the spare outboard motor, which hangs on the stern of "Svanen", is broken through by the impact. Sadly, I bring the boat to the other side of the bay Bjure-ufaerden, where there are fewer waves.

I try to loosen the retaining clips in the lee of the shore, but they don't move a millimetre. So I have to secure the outboard with the broken shaft as best I can, and we set off for the next harbour, Skellefteå. That should still take a good three hours.

INFO: SAFETY AT SEA

When you go on a cruise, and the land disappears on the horizon, it is vital to consider some basic safety rules. Time and time again, you see sailors on their yachts far out at sea without a lifejacket, sometimes even in decent winds. This does not have to be the case. The modern automatic lifejackets are not particularly thick, even if they are of a more robust design. The vest should have been serviced regularly. On the other hand, if you have ever put on a solid vest, you will know that it is worth replacing it with automatic vests. These monstrosities really hamper you on board, which is also to the detriment of safety. When I'm out single-handed, I've recently started clipping an "EPIRB" to my vest, which is a small emergency transmitter that I could use to call for help if I go overboard. There are various models on the market, some of them not so expensive. It's pretty simple: if you involuntarily fall into the water, all you have with you is what's in your pockets and dangling from your life jacket.

Second, of course, you should avoid falling into the water in the first place. If the waves get so strong that the boat starts rolling and pitching, you'd better hook yourself in with a safety line. On the forecastle, for example, when you want to work on the mast. If there is a lot of wind and waves, this will also be necessary in the cockpit. Inspect the boat for possible points where you can "pick" your line: on the mast, on the handholds on the deckhouse or similar. I would not use the railing wires as they can be too thin. Stretch lines from the cockpit to the forecastle that you can tie to. However, finding the right points for the lines is quite a fiddly job.

And speaking of rules, keep in mind the collision avoidance rules you may remember from your sailing school training. You should always overview the situation onboard and around the ship. So, if you ever go below deck to find the quiet room, make sure you have a crew member "changing the guard" or keep your stay as short as possible if you are single-handed.

The author with his life jacket on the Elbe

Also, an important rule is to always know where you are. It may be possible to enter your position on the chart once a day on the high seas. But in coastal waters, where we are cruising, you better have your position ready at all times. Nowadays, GPS receivers are cheap and built into many smartphones - I expressly appeal to use these devices. Either you note your position regularly on the paper charts, or you let the plotter record your course.

After all, it is crucial not only to see but also to be seen. The well-known radar reflector, which improves the echo of your boat on the radars of other ships and is part of the standard equipment, helps here. I also recommend using an AIS transponder, a transmitter even for small pleasure boats (they'll be called "Class B"). How often do you see big, new, expensive yachts whose skippers invest hundreds of thousands in their ship but for whom the purchase of a transponder for a few hundred Euros is too much? Yet there are lives on board, even on small yachts. As they are widely used, Pure AIS receivers can only be of limited use for your own safety. So, don't be shy. Emit an active signal with which your ship announces its own position.

Finally, one rule: if conditions become too tricky due to wind strength and waves, do not hesitate to turn around and go back. This may not be practical for an ocean crossing. But as long as you are a cruising sailor off our coasts, there is no reason to necessarily sail on if conditions at sea are no longer safe. As the saying goes: Don't let tight schedules tempt you to take unnecessary risks.

Mr. Moose says: *You humans should really be careful not to fall overboard. Because you can swim, but not as well as us moose. But you can climb back onto your boat when it's not gone. Remember: You should have a ladder that can be folded out from the water.*

In the industrial harbour approach, a German freighter gives way to us. Instead of overtaking us, the ship sits behind "Svanen" and steams with five knots behind us into the harbour. Again the industrial plant is only a "camouflage" of an attractive port, one could think, like in Husum (Sweden). Because as soon as we have passed the facilities, a small bay opens up, in which there is a lovely sailing harbour. Even better: a member of the sailing club of Skellefteå explains to us in detail what kind of facilities there are in the harbour and in the closer surroundings. First of all, the biggest attraction is the sauna, which has a window with a beautiful view of the archipelago. At 90 degrees Celsius, the rainy weather and the mishap with the outboard motor can be forgotten a little.

A beautiful sauna with a view of the archipelago

The engine was from our previous boat. The small four-stroke comes to 6 hp. I had mounted it on "Svanen" to have a motor for the inflatable dinghy. I was also curious to see what the little engine could do. In calm conditions, when there is no wind and no current, it was able to accelerate the almost four-ton Vindö to 5.5 knots, and that with only six hp. Our main engine, on the other hand, has 20 hp. So he seemed to me to be a pretty good "slack pusher", even though there was really no need for a second engine at the stern. With the correct tools our neighbour in the harbour has with him, I can dismantle the outboard together with the bracket the next day and stow it safely in the backbox. We'll see what happens to the engine in Germany. A small consolation: "Svanen" simply looks better without the auxiliary drive at the stern. After all, the designer never intended an outboard.

Skellefteå is an industrial and port city. But despite the somewhat rough atmosphere, it is cosy. The small centre has a well-stocked supermarket and a few pubs that you can visit with the sailing club's bicycles. And because there is a lot of wind again, we take a break here.

The next beat follows the triad of try, recognize, turn. Actually, it should go to a beautiful lighthouse island, but the wind blows with six Beaufort still strong over Skellefteå. We want to try it anyway. Setting the sails in the sheltered Sörfjärden in front of the harbour causes the least problem. Afterwards, we sail briskly around the industrial port. There are only a few waves here. But it should not stay like this. Because the wind blows from the east, so towards the land.

As soon as we pass the skerry Bredskär, it starts: a constant up and down. Right from the side, "Svanen" is shaken. To get 40 nautical miles north in such a swell is no fun. So an alternative port is needed. But we are already in the northern part of the Bothnian Sea, and there are not many harbours left. After a long, tedious search, I make out the port of Furögrund, not on the sea chart, but on the satellite images of Google Maps. That's where we change course now to reach the guest harbour after 20 nautical miles and four hours of sailing. The small sanctuary is beautifully situated.

The skipper of a motorboat is waiting on the shore. He follows the mooring manoeuvre with a grim face and folded arms. "Hello, this is a nice harbour here," I call out to him in English. No response. "I wonder if you could take the line sometime?" Again no response. His expression only darkens all the more. No sooner is "Svanen" moored than he mutters something in Swedish with a grim face and disappears. His companions, two ladies, also shake their heads. They get into a big car and drive away. I guess that was too much: being addressed in English by a German boat crew in Sweden. Would it have helped if I had picked up a few words of Swedish? Or was the mooring manoeuvre too unprofessional? Not really, I think. I thought it was pretty well done.

But the lovely café, accommodated in an old fisherman's house, makes it easy to forget such encounters. Furögrund is an excellent alternative port. The cake is homemade and served among antiques in the café. We also get access to electricity. Nobody in the café knows how to do that, but we can stretch several extension cables across a meadow and then "attach" them to a socket.

However, even more beautiful is the island of Antnäs-Börstskär, which we call the next day. The wind has calmed down, but it still blows just strong enough to allow us to sail comfortably. Antnäs-Börstskar is located just before Lulea, the Swedish city at the northern end of the Bothnian Sea, i.e. in Norrbotten. After eight hours and ten minutes of sailing, we moor at the only guest jetty on the island.

Today I am celebrating my birthday, and you could hardly choose a more beautiful setting for it. Birgit has lovingly decorated the ship with pennants that go across the salon. In addition, there is the birthday table in the salon, on which the gifts are piled up. And the mobile phone, which frequently rings on the quiet trip through the archipelago, where I am only too happy to receive the birthday greetings and report what a beautiful environment we are sailing in.

The jetty has four berths, there are some cottages on the shore, connected by wooden jetties, and the harbour facilities: a dry toilet and a beautiful sauna, which is wood-fired. A young Swede has approached the jetty with his girlfriend and motorboat. He helps Birgit load the stove and light the wood - it should be a nice birthday present. But even if the wood blazes for half an hour: we can't get the sauna really hot. That would require more wood, which would have to burn much longer. So it becomes a pleasant stay in a wooden room, which is heated up to 40 degrees. No sauna, but also very nice.

It gets sensitively cold at our guest jetty at night, which juts unprotected into the bay. The wind whistles through the northern waters. After all, we are roughly on the same level as Iceland. There is no electricity or other utilities here at this jetty. It was obviously more important to the municipality to equip the harbour with a sauna than electricity. Actually, I think that's quite good. And for such cases, we have also equipped "Svanen" with a diesel heater. The system starts and hisses happily while the exhaust at the stern emits small clouds at the beginning.

The jetty on the island of Antnäs-Börskar

Anyone who operates such a diesel heater at night should have CO_2-detectors fitted in their boat. Now our heater is still relatively new, so I have little fear that the combustion chamber could be faulty and pump burnt air into the boat's interior. You find reports in boating magazines about such accidents every now and then.

That's why I installed two of these little CO_2-detectors in the ship, one in the forward berth and one on the wall in the saloon. So far, they have shown nothing but "zero" - fortunately. The auxiliary heater works flawlessly and keeps the inside of the boat perfectly warm. Its pipes snake under the bench seat all the way to the forecastle. It does not capitulate even when the outside temperature drops to two or three degrees. It is a cold night with a starry sky over Antnäs-Börstskar.

6 FROM LULEÅ TO NORWAY

While "Svanen" glides in the steady wind with four knots from Antnäs-Börstskär towards Luleå, Birgit steers the ship safely. I hang on the phone. I want to book seats on the Ore Railway, also called the "Polar Express", which runs from Luleå to Narvik in Norway. This train ride is supposed to be a stopover on our sailing trip, and I imagine it is fantastic to ride the train through the forests and mountain landscapes.

Actually, the train should be back in service by now, but it is not, as the lady at the reservation hotline explains to me. Norway deals strictly with Swedish residents who want to enter in Corona times, and especially in the province of Norrbotten, the seven-day incidence is currently very high. Passenger traffic remains interrupted because of Covid-19. I think that's a shame. There is no way to get to Norway by train via Kiruna. Also, buses do not run on this route. Therefore, the only option is to look for a rental car of my own, should it go further north. This will be a small odyssey, so cumbersome is the booking. The full-bodied claims of booking portals in the net, which promise favourable rental prices, can be forgotten here in the north. That may work in Spain, but the systems all show for northern Sweden: no vehicles available - of course only after you have fought your way through the booking masks. When I finally reserved a car at the rental car company with the four red letters, we have almost reached Luleå.

The mighty icebreakers are moored at the quay

It is impressive, the fleet of icebreakers lies before us, moored at the "Isbrytarna Luleå" quay, two nautical miles from the city. In summer, "Atle", "Frej" and "Ymer" don't have much to do. Nevertheless, the lights on the ships are on, and they look as if they could cast off and begin their mission at any time. Indeed, the Sea of Bothnia doesn't freeze over entirely very often anymore. The last time it was almost completely covered by a layer of ice was in 2011. But up here, in Norrbotten, the ice comes back every winter. That's when the ice maps from the Swedish

Meteorological Institute SMHI show a thick layer of ice extending far into the northern part of the Sea of Bothnia from Luleå.

The Swedish icebreakers then have the task of not only keeping the port of Luleå navigable but also the adjacent Swedish and Finnish ports. The 105 meter long icebreakers of the "Atle class" are ready for this. They may not look as gigantic as the Russian icebreakers in Murmansk, but they look impressive with their wide helipad and high superstructures. No, hopefully, "Svanen" will not need an icebreaker this year until the Botten freezes over. Until then we want to be back in Hamburg. Shortly after the quay, we finally reach the city with the considerable guest harbour of Luleå. The facility seems a little oversized: To starboard are the local yachts, mainly motorboats, to port are the guest berths. Almost no place is occupied in the long row of free finger pontoons. So we can choose our berth calmly. At the end of the harbour, there is a petrol station. This is where most of the boats want to go because it is the weekend and the inhabitants of northern Sweden all want to get out on the water. The boats pass our stern to queue for refuelling in a long queue. Once they have their fuel, the skippers put the throttle down, often regardless of the speed limit, and leave the harbour roaring.

Luleå has its own archipelago, much like the Stockholm archipelago on a large scale. Archipelago steamers connect the countless cottages on the forested, relatively flat islands. Most importantly, residents and their guests arrive in their own boats. I would love to see the arrival in winter. Then, snowmobiles drive here to the holiday homes instead of motorboats and sailboats. We have seen the vehicles parked next to many a cottage on the way to town. I suspect they will probably give the icebreakers a wide berth.

Luleå's marina, a prominent boating business, is modern and well maintained. There is also an excellent sauna. And it is by no means rustic, as in the archipelago, but could be in a wellness hotel. You can even regulate the temperature, so it's possible to have a hot visit in the "bastu", unlike out in the archipelago, where the wooden sauna didn't get hot.

INFO: STERN ANCHOR AND MOORING LINE

In the north, you will no longer find the typical stern piles that are common in the southern and western Baltic Sea. From the Swedish south coast behind Ystad these are scarce. This is not a big deal: once you have become familiar with other "systems", you will no longer miss these impractical stakes. The easiest way to break the journey is, of course, to anchor. And there are many more anchorages in Scandinavia than on the German coast. You should always check whether the anchor is holding well. On rocky ground, you may need several attempts. If you moor in a harbour, the easiest option would be to go alongside the jetty. There is often enough space at a jetty to moor the ship at full length, especially in the fishing harbours in the north, where there are hardly any recreational boats. One line from the bow to the front, one from the stern and finally one in the middle - and your yacht is safely moored.

In the case of a jetty with finger outriggers, as in Luleå, two lines are attached from the bow, and two ropes go to the outriggers from the stern. In most cases, however, these lines have to be led slightly towards the ship's middle because the stern protrudes beyond the outriggers. The winches are ideal for this, as they can withstand a lot of pressure.

It is almost easier to moor to a stern buoy. For these, we have a hook on board to which a mooring line is attached. When you slowly pass the buoy, you can hook into the buoy's ring with a well-aimed swing. If you have practised this a bit, it is pretty straightforward. More complicated are mooring lines that extend from the jetty to the harbour's bottom, as these have to be picked up at the front near the jetty. The trick, then, is to keep the boat reasonably in position while the line is led aft. But once this has been achieved, you can very comfortably tie the line to your stern cleat.

Stern anchors are not elaborate either, replacing buoys, stern stakes and other aids in many northern harbours. You just have to drop the anchor in time before you approach your berth so that the anchor chain does not point too tightly downwards. If the anchor grips well, the job is done quickly. But if it doesn't grab, you'll have to repeat the mooring manoeuvre. Or you can tie up the boat temporarily and then go into the harbour basin armed with diving goggles to dig in your anchor. We have observed this unusual manoeuvre, which I am not inclined to do, not so rare in Scandinavia.

Mr. Moose says: *I have had a lot of fun watching you dock. The most important thing is that you try to do it calmly. One thing at a time, don't stress unnecessarily. If you take your time, you will be able to moor your boat in unknown harbours.*

On any yachting voyage, you will sooner or later need equipment for your boat, be it fenders, a halyard or even an anchor. But what struck us in Scandinavia is the lack of dealers for ship accessories. Those in need of equipment could run into problems. Indeed, there is an excellent outfitter in Kalmar, in

Vaxholm, and in Luleå. Later we also meet a ship chandler in Finland and on the Åland Islands. That was it. We didn't come across any other such shops. And even in the places where the coastal handbook still lists outfitters, they had closed. No wonder a country like Sweden, where the internet is very prevalent, has even less retail than Germany. Orders are placed online and then usually delivered by parcel service. Another reason is that the shops, which do exist in the greater Stockholm area, are located on arterial roads and are not easily accessible by bus & train, let alone by boat.

However, it is interesting that new shipping methods are also emerging: An online shipper of marine accessories in Stockholm has its goods delivered by boat. After ordering, the customer can choose a time slot when this boat will come to him at the berth in the archipelago. A rather original model, but one that has yet to prove itself. So we strike at the ship chandler and equip "Svanen" with a new "grappling hook", as I also call the boat hooks and some cordage. As we are planning the trip to Norway, I will try to negotiate a discount for the berth. The manager agrees but still wants to take the equivalent of 20 instead of 25 Euros per night. For Sweden, this is nevertheless not that expensive. And we don't have to pay with the curious app the port uses. He has converted the car parking app of Luleå. Instead of parking space for your car, you book the berth for the ship, elaborate registration included. "It's not a good system," the harbour master admits when I pay with my card at his cash desk.

Luleå is a pretty, well-arranged little town that, with just under 80,000 inhabitants, is about the size of Flensburg. Up here, that's indeed something. The city centre is situated on a peninsula, around which the river "Luleälven" flows. On the southern side, there is the colossal guest harbour. On the northern side, there is a smaller one. But to reach it, you have to pass under a low bridge, which is not possible for sailing yachts like ours. In between is a pleasant pedestrian zone with many shops and restaurants. While the southern side has been modernized with many new buildings built on top of the old cargo handling facilities, the northern harbour looks deserted. The houses have rough concrete facades and face away from the water. A wide street seals off the shore. At most, the cultural centre around the "Norbottensteatern" brings some life. But on this Sunday, the bars are all closed.

After a long walk, we find a Greek restaurant near the south harbour. And even if the "Google" rating of this restaurant is quite mixed, and there are rather international standard dishes, the food is good, and the restaurant is worth a visit. Maybe you can't always put all your eggs in one basket on reviews. Nevertheless, Luleå seems somewhat deserted at the northern harbour and overall. And also, some empty shop window facades show: It is not really "buzzing" in the capital of Norrbotten. But we are already very far in the north. By car, we would be 902 kilometres away from Stockholm. That is about as far as the distance from Hamburg to Salzburg.

And now we want to go even further north. After two days, the car is ready at the station in Luleå. While I take over the key, Birgit is interviewed by the local newspaper about the Swedish railway system. Well, up here, there are only a few lines and stations for passenger traffic. We would like to use the railway, but the trains to Norway are not running. And so we roll out of town in a "Kia Sorento". After the many weeks at sea, it feels pretty unusual to be on the road with a car. But it is also quite comfortable. The switches for ventilation and music are quickly found on the dashboard, which is strangely cheaply made of plastic in contrast to the impressively large car. The Kia is a hybrid car. If you charge it at a socket - a standard household socket will do overnight - you can drive 50 kilometres on pure electric power. This is not a fantastic value, but it is nice to have a hybrid as a rental car.

We drive through the seemingly endless forests towards Kiruna and pass the Arctic Circle. In contrast to the hustle and bustle that prevails in Norway on the European Road 6 north at the "Polarsirkelsenteret", this is a little less spectacular. A huge sign announces the Arctic Circle, but the associated souvenir shop is closed. There is hardly any traffic up here, we don't find a petrol station to make a stop either. A few hours later, we pass Kiruna. After that, the landscape changes. Before it was mainly dense forests we drove through, now plateaus follow. When we come to the lake Torneträsk, the mountain ranges begin. The 70-kilometre long lake lies quietly between the mountains; only one or two boats are on it, there are a few villages on its southern shore. The road winds beautifully along the lake shore.

Finally, it happens: In the vastness of the northern Swedish countryside, Mr Moose makes his grand entrance. I almost slam on the brakes when I see him standing at the edge of the forest out of the corner of my eye. The car stops. Mr Moose is not impressed. Very slowly, I back the vehicle up, metre by metre. Then we are standing next to him: a moose, large and majestic. He looks at us somewhat sceptically. He moves his big head back and forth. He kicks a little with its front legs. And then, suddenly, he makes a leap into the forest and disappears between the trees. The car that stopped for him didn't seem that interesting. Goodbye, Mr Moose.

But it wasn't the only moose we encountered on the drive to Norway. A few kilometres further on, I see another one. Or is it the same one? No, Mr Moose can't run through the undergrowth that fast after all. Maybe it's his cousin? Perhaps it's Mrs. Moose? You can't really tell through the forest. But this specimen also disappears quickly.

And then there is a particular highlight for all moose lovers: suddenly, there is a moose in the middle of the road. Just like that. Another hard brake and the car stops again. But the moose is not at all afraid of that. But he takes to his heels. Nevertheless, I am happy: I met Mr. Moose three times on this day, which is a reason for joy. After a few hours, we reach the Norwegian border. We are already happy about the uncomplicated entry until we have to stop at a checkpoint of the Norwegian army, six kilometres behind the border. The Swedish cars drive one after the other into huge tents. The country shows in the Corona summer 2021 that it takes the controls very seriously.

Then it's our turn. If we speak Swedish or Norwegian, the soldier wants to know. I shake my head and tell him that we can only speak English or German. Then his expression brightens. He scans the codes on both smartphones and is happy that we are vaccinated and can enter the country.

The drive down from the mountains to the sea in Norway is spectacular. We stop in a bay in the small town of Bjerkvik. The first thing we notice here on the coast is the extensive tidal range. The beaches are wide, the sea comes and goes. The jetties that reach into the water here are very high. Fascinated, I stand on the shore: We have reached the coast on the other side of the "European North Sea" from the Bothnian Sea in a good day's drive. We spend the night in the very cheap airport hotel of Narvik before we drive to the Lofoten the next day.

After almost every bend in the road on the E10 that leads to the archipelago, there is a new view of the mountains that drop steeply and rockily into the sea. The landscape is entirely different from the Bothnian Sea. We move into the "Vandrarhem" in Kabelvag. The distance from the Norwegian border at Riks-gränsen to this small village on the Lofoten is 250 kilometres. We pay a proud price of 130 Euros per night for a youth hostel.

But on the other hand, this was the cheapest offer on the entire Lofoten. On the other hand, the big room offers a comfort that we are not used to after weeks on our ship, including a breakfast buffet. But not that you get this wrong: As a change, the Vandrarhem is very appealing, but for the entire tour, I would not want to give up my own ship and the freedom to enjoy every day onboard.

When the superstructures of these beacons are not
needed, they are stored in the depot

One question comes to mind: Would one also visit the
Lofoten by sailing boat? That would be a dream and finally, in
the neighbouring place Svolvaer with its big harbour, there are
also some sailing ships. These are all big yachts with a length of
14 metres and more that already outwardly give the impression
that they can sail safely even in stormy conditions. But the route
from northern Germany across the Skagerrak and then up the
long Norwegian coast is very long and runs in unprotected
sections.

On the Lofoten, most villages are pretty touristy. If you drive
to Henningsvaer, our Kia rental car takes us there purely electri-
cally, you join a queue of cars and campers. They all want to visit
the pretty fishing village around the harbour basin and calls itself
the "Venice of the North". Well, the "Venice comparison" can be
used for many places. We know that. I'll just say, "Hamburg has

more bridges than Venice." Did you know? Still, the "Venice of the Lofoten" is pretty to look at, and it's fun to mingle with the other tourists.

But the natural sensation of this five-day excursion to Norway is the weather: the sun is shining all the time, there is hardly a cloud in the sky. On one day, fog came up from the sea and dipped the landscape in wadding white, which was soon dissolved by the sun again.

Norway like in a picture book in Henningsvaer

On the way back, we treat ourselves to a stopover in a simple hotel that specializes in truckers on the bypass. Kiruna will lose its town centre in a few years, as ore is to be mined there as well. Therefore a new centre is being built in front of the town. Nothing will be invested in buildings that will only remain standing for a few more years, and accordingly, the mining town is not attractive. We return to our boat to Luleå, which we are only too happy to reach. There are still many exciting sights up here. If we hadn't met Mr Moose on the road a few times, there would still be a way to meet him: Near Luleå there is the highly recommended animal park "Cape Wild", only ten kilometres from the guest harbour. There you can visit not only some moose, but also reindeer. During a tour of the park, the animal keepers can tell you a lot about the life of the moose. They know much more than I can write in this book.

And also, the North Cape is not that far away from Luleå, or the forests of Finland, but now we continue the journey "on our own keel" again.

7 THE ROUTE TO HAPARANDA

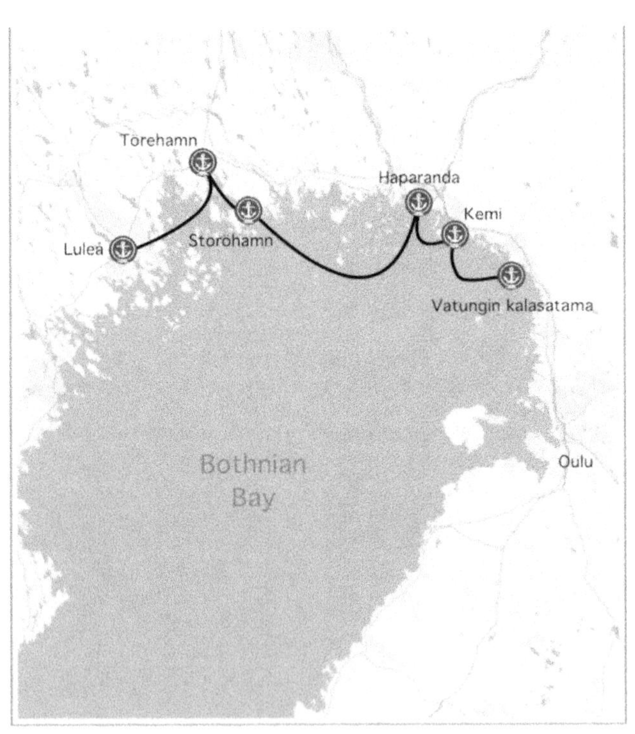

We first leave Luleå on the main route to the north through the industrial harbour. Iron ore is loaded here, which the ore railway from Kiruna brings to the edge of the Bothnian Sea. There is a lot of dust as we pass the quay of the loading facility, where a bulk carrier is being loaded. And there is also quite a lot of shipping traffic: big cargo ships, pilot boats, and a sea rescue vessel pass by. So we are glad to turn onto a course that branches off directly to the north and zigzags through the archipelago.

Today we will go to the northernmost buoy of the Baltic Sea at the village of Töre. To do this, we drive up a bay into which the small river Töreälven flows. I thought for a long time whether this side trip was actually worthwhile. But there it is in front of us, the often described buoy, in the middle of the harbour of Töre. It has a wide edge where yachts can moor. One can even climb up. If you put a form into a mailbox at the buoy, you will receive a certificate by mail. It proves that you have really reached the buoy. This clever action was thought up by the operator of the camping site at the harbour. The certificates are also sent from there. A sailor is already moored at the nearby jetty, whom we have met before in some ports before Luleå. The friendly gentleman from Gothenburg is also sailing up the Swedish coast to Haparanda. Actually, he wanted to go to Norway, but Corona had upset his plans in his plans when the borders remained closed for the time being. And so he finds himself up here in Töre.

To be honest, I find this place a bit unattractive. Nothing against an empty port, where no freighter is moored anymore. But somehow, the buoy can't fascinate me. But it is not the destination of our journey, which is called "from Hamburg to Haparanda", and not "from Hamburg to Töre". And so we leave the harbour after the extensive inspection of the buoy. We follow the fairway southwards again. Some red buoys alternate with a row of green ones. The banks are wooded and relatively flat. The route is - you will guess - simply beautiful.

This is it, the northernmost buoy in the Baltic Sea

We call at the harbour of Storöhamn. However, this is not a place for leisure skippers. Here several fishing cutters lie at a long concrete jetty. Behind them are buildings for fish processing. There are no supply possibilities, but there is space to moor in front of another sailing yacht. Actually, this is a very original berth between fishing vessels. There is actually always something to see, unlike anchoring in front of a skerry. That's why I would call us "harbour friends". However, mosquitoes do not stop at such harbours and come onto the ships, which we should notice only too well.

INFO: IN THE LAND OF MOSQUITOES

So far, the buzzing pests have largely spared us. That in itself is amazing. We had far more to do with the mosquitoes from previous trips to Scandinavia. But up here, in the flat, wooded waters of Norboten, there is no more pardon: the mosquitoes are coming. The most important thing now is to get the ship tight. Because the tiny mosquitoes manage amazingly well to crawl through the most minor cracks. The result: when you lie in your bunk at night, you can hear the pests buzzing closer. And if you catch one, you'll quickly have a bloodstain on the wall. So: The hatches must be closed. You will still need some ventilation openings. On "Svanen", for example, there are the deck vents, which have already been fitted with grilles. But these "air holes" are much too small to provide ventilation in a harbour with not much wind.

Therefore we leave the passage to the deck open and install a mosquito net there. This has to be meticulously taped to really keep the critters out. I also have the good fortune to switch the auxiliary heating to ventilation on "Svanen". Then the unit just sucks in air in the cockpit, secured by a grille, and blows it into the ship, making for a pleasant draught. And if there's no other way: good old "Autan" also helps on the shores of the Bothnian Sea, as does its cousin "Anti-Brumm". When rubbing it in, however, you should not forget any part of the skin. So I often made the experience that even denim does not keep the animals away. Fortunately, this is not a problem on the open sea, but only in the harbour. Which animal is most common in Scandinavia? The mosquito, of course.

Mr. Moose says: *Terrible. These mosquitoes are really awful. Almost as bad as flies. We moose don't like them at all. My tip for you: Stay away from the dry land when there are many mosquitoes. We moose like to take a few steps into the water and stand there. That way, we have more peace and quiet from the pests.*

We are now sailing the last section to Haparanda. That is only 27 nautical miles. First, we go around the peninsula Skagsudden and then continue across the open sea, just to the east. Again I search the archipelago for Mr Moose. This should be his exact territory, according to the TV report. But there are no moose on the shores of the small islands. But maybe in the water? His head might look big on land, but in the water, it's quite small? So I look closely, search the surface of the water. No, there is no Mr Moose to be seen up here, just before Haparanda. That's a pity, but at least I got to see him in the forests just before Norway.

The pretty island Seskarö also has to be circumnavigated to the south, as the bridge that connects it with the mainland is only 10,7 metres high. But then it goes precisely to the north, and slowly the goal pushes itself into the visible map section of the plotter: "Haparanda Hamn" comes closer.

I had previously read a lot of nice but also disparaging about the border town. The destination is boring, it says in some cruise reports. Let's hope not. But after visiting the northernmost buoy,

I am prepared. The most suitable description was given by the travel guide "Lonely Planet", which compares Haparanda with its neighbouring town Tornio in Finland. Tornio had interesting pubs, a kind of art scene and a lot of life, but what had Haparanda? Not much more than the world's most giant Ikea in a shopping centre on the ring road. Well, let's get to the bottom of that.

The Clubhouse in Haparanda Harbour

We moor in Haparanda Hamn, about ten kilometres from the actual town. This is because the river that separates the city from Tornio, the wide Torne älv, also offers small harbours in the town, but with a draught of one metre, it is too shallow for us, and with bridges that only have a clearance of six metres it is entirely unsuitable. But "Haparanda Hamn" is no tragedy as a destination. The harbour has been extended and now offers many jetties for recreational skippers. I think the pier is even very well developed.

But the attraction is the clubhouse of the sailing club, which is housed in a yellow villa directly behind the harbour. A club member shows us around the house and tells us about sailors who come from far away. There are sanitary facilities, the sauna in the basement and lounges, and the heart, the magnificent "flag room": hundreds of pennants hang from the ceiling here. New lines have to be stretched across the room to take up new pennants. Countless sailing crews have hung up their club flags or those of their hometowns, often immortalizing their names on the banners. I don't have to look very hard to spot a few Hamburg flags among them. This gives the sailing port a unique international flair. It is, after all, the destination of many adventurous sailors who have not shied away from the long journey across the Bothnian Sea.

Flags from all over Europe hang in the clubhouse

The next day we wait at the harbour for the minibus that is supposed to drive into town. It arrives, and because I now know how to take a bus in Sweden, I have long since installed the appropriate app and paid for two tickets. The friendly driver roars off with his load of guests and goes on the Europe Road and directly into the centre of Haparanda. No, we don't get off at the shopping centre with the legendary Ikea, but first, take a look at downtown.

The striking focal point is the "Stadshotelet". Here, part of the former, magnificent town hall was converted into a hotel. The 3-star hotel has a nostalgic flair both inside and out, enhanced by the high ceilings and the old furniture. The administration now resides in a flat, functional building next to the town hall. Unfortunately, the "Lonely Planet" travel guide is right: the city centre really doesn't offer many shops. Diagonally opposite the town hall, you can order lunch in a somewhat better snack bar. A short walk leads to the riverbank, where a pretty park stretches along the banks of Torne älv. I stop, impressed: Finland lies on the other side. A mighty railway bridge and a road bridge cross the river. Behind the bridge is the modern wellness hotel "Cape East", which the Lonely Planet writes has the world's largest sauna area. Whatever prompted the authors to endow Haparanda with superlatives, the complex is beautiful, but it certainly doesn't have the world's largest sauna area.

Let's not forget the Haparanda railway station. It is impressively large and has a significant past. On the outskirts of the town to the south lies the vast stone building that was erected in 1915 for the new railway line. This ran along Norbotten's coast and was also an important European connection. The trains went from Sweden to Russia, to which Finland belonged until 1917. Passengers had to change trains at the border station, or the wagons were reeled in for the Russian broad-gauge network. In 1917 Vladimir Ilyich Ulyanov passed through here. "Lenin" travelled from Zurich to St. Petersburg, passing through Sweden and Finland by land, as the journey across the Baltic Sea to the south seemed too dangerous for him. The route took him via Haparanda. As his wagon was sealed, he could not get off at the northernmost station of his journey. Passenger traffic continued to pass the monumental building until 1992 when the line was discontinued due to lack of demand. The rails are now only for freight traffic on the bridge over the river - many railway fans like to take photos of it. After all, on April 1, 2021, passenger traffic between the more southern bottom and Haparanda resumed. Here is the end of the line, because the trains do not go on, but back.

Before the Corona crisis, Haparanda and Tornio tried to market themselves as a Swedish-Finnish borderless twin city. The pandemic killed this initiative: the Finns have reintroduced the border post and carefully examine all travellers from Sweden if they are allowed to pass at all. From the corrugated iron buildings on the border, you can see how Corona is weighing heavily on the Schengen area.

Now, what about the Ikea? In the seventies, Ikea had a unique advertising logo: it showed a moose. The Swedish national animal, so to speak, as a logo next to the Ikea lettering. At that time, at least in Germany, the company also called itself "the impossible furniture store from Sweden". The moose made it very likeable. But Mr Moose can't be seen anywhere in Haparanda's Ikea today either. By the way: the moose still exists today as an advertising logo. My Volvo dealer near Hamburg has a moose on his logo. It is a Swedish car (even though my model was built in Belgium). The dealer stuck it on the boot lid, a small sticker with Mr Moose. But back to Ikea.

It's true: Haparanda got a gigantic shopping centre on the European Road. It's massive by Norrbotten standards. Accordingly, Ikea is also giant. In 2006, the company inaugurated the building with exactly 24,254 square metres of space, which is open every day of the week. Let's compare: the not exactly small store in Hamburg-Schnelsen has 18,000 square meters, the one in

Moorfleet 20,000. Indeed, point victory for Haparanda, at least in comparison with Hamburg.

In Berlin, however, there is an Ikea in Lichtenberg with an area of 43,000 square meters. The largest of the 430 stores that the group operates worldwide was opened in Manila in the Philippines and had an incredible 60,000 square meters of sales space. To sum up: The Ikea in Haparanda is downright ludicrously large for a town of 10,000 people. It is the only one of its kind on the north coast of the Bothnian Sea. The department store with its restaurant seems to supply the whole region with furniture and household goods. After all, Ikea is strategically located on the border between Sweden and Finland, even if the border is now more difficult to cross. And 50 per cent of this store's turnover comes from cross-border trade, as can be read in the local newspaper's archives, which of course reports touchingly about "its" Ikea. And five to six per cent is accounted for by the restaurant. It's a good thing we've already eaten in the centre, what's on the tablets here is hardly any different from what's on offer in Hamburg-Schnelsen. However, Haparanda is not to be found among the most extensive branches of the group.

Our minibus rumbles comfortably back down the road to Haparanda Hamn. On the way, a drunken Swede tries to describe the region's beauties to me. This is funny, but you can only understand him if you get very close to him. He speaks English, but the pronunciation suffers from his alcohol level. I am quite happy when the bus turns the corner at the harbour and I wish the man, who wanted to be friendly but was too drunk for that, a good journey.

Not the biggest, but the northernmost Ikea in the world

Another division of tasks has emerged between Haparanda and Tornio in Finland: Haparanda has the sailing port, Tornio the industrial port. It is impressively large, as we discover the next day when we cross the border between the two countries, which runs directly in front of the 2.5-kilometre-long port facilities. And here, the double city Haparanda / Tornio really has a superlative to offer: The largest wood processing plant in the northern hemisphere is to be put into operation by the Metsä Group. The plant is said to have a total of 500 jobs from 2023, as the company had just announced. For those who are now worried that the huge forests of Lapland could all disappear without replacement in the plant, the company has some unctuous words: biodiversity will be safeguarded and the positive influence of forests on the climate will be expanded, said Metsä CEO Ilkka Hämälä when presenting the plans. Wood processing is of great importance to the environment. After all, wood stores a large amount of CO2. They are professionals, I notice, at Metsä they know how to express themselves adequately. I keep my fingers crossed for

Hämälä's plans and, of course, for the preservation of biodiversity.

The clocks are set forward one hour, and we find it exciting to pass a time zone with "Svanen". But the real excitement is much more the strong wind that blows from the north with six Beaufort into our reefed sails. This is not a tragedy on this somewhat rainy day, as the archipelago in front of the two towns keeps the waves out. But navigation is very demanding here, as the fairways between the skerries are pretty shallow. You also have to get used to the electronic sea chart for Finland, which has a different display than the Swedish one. The colouring of the depth contours is no longer as nicely adjustable to two metres as before. It is rather a bit chaotic. Of course, you can see the lines, but the colored areas seem to follow a different logic. It goes on like this until Kemi, the next town and the first port we call in Finland. The water is not deep enough before the entrance, according to the map, when coming from the east. Some sailors in front of us seem to speak for the opposite. We follow the yachts and actually reach the harbour safely.

Kemi is a very friendly guest harbour. At first, nobody knows: We are asking in two restaurants and a café for the harbour master. Finally, we find what we are looking for in the fourth restaurant. It's a good thing that English is spoken here, too. The Finnish language can always surprise you: It consists of extended, flowing expressions that sound very melodic. But unlike Swedish, there is no longer any way to intuitively grasp word meanings.

The strong wind increases a bit more so that we stay two nights in the harbour. The harbour master now goes to the promenade and raises a huge German flag, which flies next to the Finnish one.

"You just planted a nice flag, though," we say to him.

"But yes. We are glad that you are here," it comes back in English.

"So do we. But is it so special that Germans are moored here?"

"Oh yes. There have been two boats from Germany here already this year. That's a lot. You're the third boat now, and I want everyone in town to know that."

Haparanda or the Bothnian Sea - there don't seem to be many sailors from our northern German area coming to Kemi. A little later, a yacht from Poland moors, which is why the diligent harbour master went to the flagpoles again to hoist the Polish flag.

A tour of the town of 20,000 inhabitants shows that many houses date from the 1950s, as Kemi was pretty much destroyed in the Second World War. The townhouse is impressive: It looks like a high-rise building from the seventies, looks entirely Finnish, with its massive roof, which houses a water reservoir. But the 15-storey construction was completed in 1940 and survived the war. Some houses in the city could be architectural models because they have precise shapes and large windows.

The downtown, which seems quite large, looks very US-American with its right-angled streets. "Downtown" is a bit run down. Not every building has a business that is still open. One bright spot: On the edge of downtown is the first "Hessburger" I've come across in a long time. This Finnish fast-food chain once tried to gain a foothold in Germany and operated three branches in Hamburg at once. But after a few years, they gave up, closed again and left Germany. Maybe I remember them a bit nostalgi-cally: the hamburger with the onion rings doesn't taste that great anymore. So back to the charming waterfront and the marina.

The German flag is set in the harbour of Kemi

As we leave Kemi, the course heads Southwest for the first time in weeks. We sail out the bow of the Bothnian Sea. Actually, the trip should go to Röyttä, a much-praised archipelago island. But again, the wind blows with 18 knots and then still directly from the front. The crossing is difficult in the fairway in front of the harbour of Kemi. The waves take on quite a size in front of the port, they are probably over a metre high.

So I take out the tablet in the swaying cockpit and replan. The new destination is the port Vatungin kalasatama. The ride across the wave is now surprisingly stable, although exhausting. "Svanen" is making very decent speed at over six knots. Vatungin kalasatama is described in the coastal handbook as a spacious leisure harbour with a campsite. That didn't seem to work out that way up here in the northern Bottenwiek. The café is closed, there are no campers, the utilities are locked, the guest jetty has been dismantled. Instead, a couple of wind turbines, located right on the harbour, are noisily swinging their blades. Apparently, running a recreational haven up here hasn't paid off. A friendly fisherman tells us that the port now mainly serves the aquacultures off the coast.

"That's where I go out," he says, pointing to the aquaculture that sits in the bay off the harbour. "But only when the weather is calm. Then we get up to 500 kilos of salmon a day from the plant."

"Who eats the salmon that comes here?"

"Oh, it's picked up by the refrigerated truck here at the port. All over Lapland, our fish is delivered from Vatungin kalasatama and we are proud of that."

Then he shows his latest technical achievement: it is an echo sounder for the fishing hook. With it, he surveys the sea area around the harbour. The official nautical charts are simply too inaccurate, he criticizes. Indeed, his tablet displays the image like a fish finder. Next, the fisherman tells me he wants to buy a big Garmin device to do his personal surveying even better. I don't want to dampen his enthusiasm - I'll keep to myself that I'm not at all happy with the old Garmin onboard "Svanen".

8 OULU, THE BIG CITY IN THE NORTH

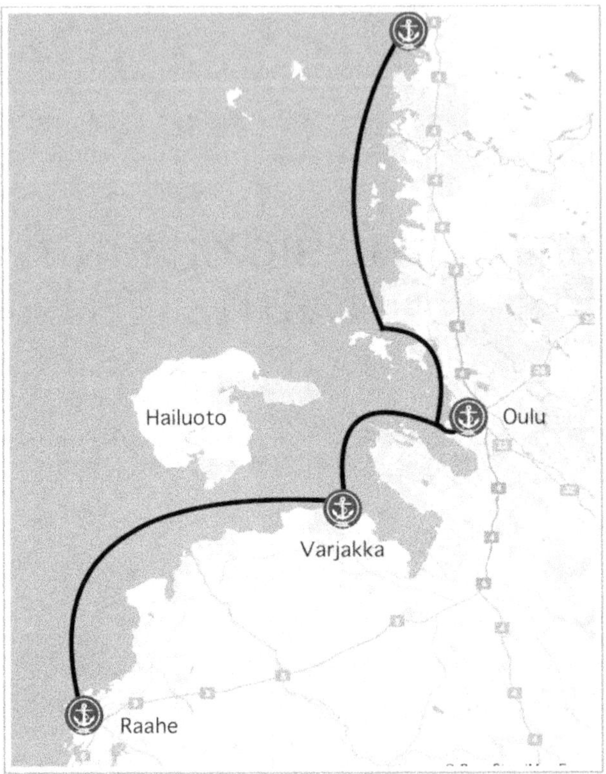

Even if one comes from the sea or sails along the coast, big cities announce themselves. Slowly the development on the shore increases, smaller harbours come in denser order, the traffic on the water increases. This is the case on the Elbe when sailing towards Hamburg or approaching Warnemünde. I always find the transition between land and city or sea and city fascinating: it's not yet the city you're sailing into, but you've already left the open ocean. In the case of Oulu, it's like that when you approach from the north, passing between the Mustakari peninsula and the island of Heta Kari.

Already from a distance, you can see the harbour with its

pilot station. A friendly appearing guest harbour, where many sailing boats are moored. Only a few miles later, we reach the next jetty in Kiviniemi. Some sailors are in front of us, motorboats are darting back and forth. The weather is fine. We left the small harbour of Vatunginnoka in the morning. The distance to Oulu is about 40 nautical miles, for which we need eight hours - so we are on our way very quickly.

Oulu is shielded from the sea by a multitude of islands. As we are sailing close to the coast, we have to pass through a narrow passage, barely a nautical mile long, at Takkulannlokka. Thereafter we land in a sheltered bay, where there is a lot of activity. It is Friday afternoon, the weekend is starting, and many Finns are out with their boats. This is another difference between big cities near the sea and small towns: You meet more leisure sailors on the coast. Even this area on the doorstep must be brilliant for the sailing inhabitants of Oulu because they can get out on the water in a protected area even in inclement weather.

About six nautical miles, you sail along with the city's suburbs before the harbour entrance comes. On both sides of the fairway are port facilities, cranes, container bridges and industrial plants. Immediately one notices: Everything here is clean and spruced up. If there ever were industrial scrap and fallow areas in Oulu, they have been meticulously cleaned up. The harbour advertises itself with a neon sign on a grain silo.

The harbour in the centre of Oulu with the "Oulon"

The waterway becomes narrower and narrower until we leave the industrial harbour area and approach the city. Now the first guest harbour Johannsoni Raanta appears on the port side. The disadvantage: the dock is located on a peninsula, and the way to the city would be a bit long with 3,3 kilometres. In addition, the city harbour attracts with its central location directly in Oulu. However, we could not foresee that Johannsoni Raanta might not have been such a bad choice. So we leave the harbour on the port side and sail into the heart of the city. By the way, we reach a mark when we arrive in Oulu, as I calculate: 1125 nautical miles we are already underway on this trip. So we have passed the mark of 2000 kilometres on board "Svanen".

Between huge motor yachts, there are also some sailboats at the jetty. A friendly Finn is just leaving, but he takes his time and shows us his place in perfect English. The sanitary facilities are built into an old wooden storehouse in true style. You get the key in the next bar, where you also pay. There is life everywhere: In the harbour, on the green in the park in front of it, on the marketplace at the other side of the harbour. Friday evening in summer in a big city with 209,000 inhabitants in Finland, which is completely unknown to us. We may have heard of Lulea on the Swedish side, but Oulu? In Swedish, the city is also called Uleåborg. So it is about the same size as Lübeck. Although it also has traditional industries such as wood processing, paper manufacturing and a steel mill, Oulu has made a name in Scandinavia with its hi-tech economy. The university also bears are share of this, the largest in the country after the universities in Helsinki. After all, the Finnish capital is 629 kilometres to the south. The Kauppatori marketplace is a hive of activity. Stalls are open. There are dozens of restaurants, bars and cafés with packed terraces. In the restaurant "Kahvilamakasiinit" young musicians perform. Each plays only three songs, then it's the next gig. Compared to Lulea in Sweden, there are differences. Oulu seems more modern, tidier, has wide shopping streets in which, unlike in Sweden, not a single shop is empty. There is also a beautiful market hall at the marketplace, the "Kauppahalli". And there seems to be no end to the number of pubs, as we discover while strolling along the main street Kauppurienkatu and its side streets. After a long cruise, it is good to be in a "real" big city. One of Oulu's landmarks is particularly original: the 2.20 metre high bronze statue Toripolliisi, which depicts a rather plump little market policeman. The Finnish artist Kaarlo Mikkonen created it in 1987. And even the police apparently like it so much that they have put stickers of the market policeman on the windows of the nearest police station.

The sun sets in the centre of Oulu

Now, it is said of Finland that once people start partying, it is hard for them to stop. They are even more consistent than their Scandinavian neighbours. And Oulu is in a celebratory mood this summer evening. The harbour on the island of Kiikeli is a party hotspot, as we discover as time approaches. Corona or not, it's getting crowded on the meadows behind the harbour, including a beach. Large quantities of beer are being brought in by visitors, and the noise level is rising hour by hour. It doesn't get very dark in Oulu, even at the beginning of August. There we are now, lying in our Vindö, after a long stroll through the city. At three o'clock in the night, I am startled when an open-air music system is put into operation right in front of us on the jetty, cheered by many alcoholic Finns. And what's blaring out of it? Tunes in Finnish, the party people are singing along enthusi-astically. I stick my head out of the cabin. The sky is already bright again. It has not become emptier on the meadows around the harbour. There's no question about it: we're moored in the party hotspot of Oulu. Anyone who longs for life on a cruise through the north will be well served here - perhaps more than they would like.

The following day I decide to participate in the online boom in Finland. I buy a prepaid card at an "R-Kiosk" to use the network permanently. The waitress in the kiosk knows her way around surprisingly well. I leave the shop with a "Hypernetti" card from the provider DNA. So there is Hypernet instead of Internet, I like that already. The card costs around 21 euros and is valid for one month. The best thing is that it is unlimited - no volume, no pseudo flat rate, but Internet without any limitation. Onboard, I plug it into the second sim card slot of the smartphone and turn on the Internet radio, which I rarely turn off. Now there's online music, plus news and streaming TV. Those were the days ten years ago. I bought a Danish prepaid card with a strictly limited volume just to call up the weather report via the Internet. Loading the seven different weather models with the "PredictWind" app is no longer a problem with Hypernetti, nor is streaming my favourite smooth jazz station from California at the same time, which sounds from the Bluetooth speaker on board.

You could spend a lot of time in Oulu, the city attracts with old houses and modern architecture, with many museums and its lively shopping streets. But the prospect of staying in the middle of the party mile doesn't appeal to us.

"We'd like to leave," I say to the harbormaster in the bar, standing behind the counter.

"That's too bad. Why is that?"

"Well, it's a little noisy here at night."

"A little noisy? All hell breaks loose here at night. I wouldn't last a night there," she confesses. "That's when you should really leave." Unless you sleep all day and then be fit for the next night, she adds.

Carefully we cast off in the late afternoon, move the Vindö gently backwards, turn and drive out of the city harbour. It's supposed to be a short jump, an afternoon cruise. The problem: There are few harbours with sufficient draught up here, as the sea off Oulu is shallow. The port of Varjakka, which is 17 nautical miles away, could just about fit our shallow draft of 1.30 metres, as I discovered after studying the marine charts. We take the route around the peninsula with the airport, the second-largest in Finland. A long queue of cars is waiting for a ferry to a large island off Oulu, which we pass. We follow a route through the fairway, which is excellent with a draft of 1.80 metres. There is a scraping on the ground, and boom - we sit up behind the ferry. It seems to be sand, and the next wave lifts us up to get free again. But this route doesn't seem to be very trustworthy, because of 1.80 meters. A little later, we have reached the entrance to the harbour. The entry is exceptionally shallow. The depth sounder shows 0.0 meters. But no scratching is to be heard. It is just enough. Our "Svanen" is the most giant boat in the harbour, where otherwise only small motorboats and two tiny sailboats are moored. We stop at a finger jetty, from which the ship half protrudes.

INFO: ARCHIPELAGO HIGHWAYS IN FINLAND

We first encountered them in Sweden, the trim dotted lines on the nautical chart called "Recommended Small Craft Routes". They are convenient for accurate route planning. I called them "archipelago highways" at Gothenburg because they were really crowded like highways, especially on weekends. Bow to bow, the boats there pulled north and south along the coast, the route pointing a safe way through the archipelago. In Finland, it is different. Two German sailors had already warned us in a

Swedish harbour. In Finland, these routes are marked with very different draughts.

If you plan your route and follow the lines on the map, you will sometimes see how a fairway with a draught of two metres suddenly ends up in one with a draught of 1.40 metres. And some supposed shortcuts on the map behind an island only have a draught of one metre - and are therefore no longer navigable for most keelboats. This is because the entire Finnish coast on the Bothnian Sea is much shallower than on the Swedish side.

However, sometimes the lines of the routes are shown without any indication of draught, at least on the electronic charts on some plotters and on the nautical charts available for purchase from the open-source solution "OpenCPN". The draught must first be requested by clicking on the route and then displaying the information for each section separately. Only in the Garmin Bluechart maps could we find the info next to each path. So you can't just follow a route like in Sweden. You have to verify beforehand if the draft is sufficient on the planned route, especially if you plan electronically with the plotter. And for many boats with a deeper keel, this eliminates many paths.

Mr. moose says: *Haha, roads, routes and regulations everywhere. That's not for us moose. We walk and swim along where we like, just like that. But of course, we don't have a keel to drag through the water either. That's why you should always make sure it's deep enough up here. Use your echo sounders!*

In Varjakka, the mooring fee of around 14 euros, which is moderate for Scandinavia, is paid in the harbour café. There is actually everything there: shower with toilet and a sauna, plus the lovely café, which is housed in a pretty old archipelago steamer, the "Hailuoto", which was laid on stones on the shore and can be visited. Apart from a few camper vans and a handicraft shop, that's it for the little harbour's attractions. The following day the wind whistles with six Beaufort over the sanctuary, which lies very exposed in front of Oulu. Also, the wave in front of the pier is strong. Drizzle makes for poor visibility. I don't want to go over the next flat spot in this weather, which we will inevitably have to pass on our way south along the route mentioned above. We are stuck between two shallows near Hailuoto Island.

But there is enough to do in the small port. There are two video calls with Germany, and I can use the new "Hypernetti" card for that. The LTE connection is excellent. In Finland, the network often reaches far out on the coast. After a snack in the lovely harbour café, the sauna is heated up. Through the windows, you have a nice view of the sea in front of the small harbour. The whitecaps fly over the sea, while the sauna stove crackles and the hot air from the infusion rises. It is strange how big "Svanen" is compared to the other boats in the harbour. But it fits. The sauna improves the gloomy mood. In Finland's north, people know how to help themselves even in summer when the weather doesn't play along.

South of Oulu, there is also an animal park, the lovely little "Escurial". There are mainly birds, horses and also reindeer. And, we are in Finland, also a sauna for the visitors. Unfortunately, the only thing missing from the small park are moose. That's why we're skipping "Escurial" on this visit.

When we went on our honeymoon a few years ago, Birgit and I went skiing in Finland in the middle of winter. There, of course, we also encountered moose. Not in the wild, on the edge of the ski slopes. That might have been a bit too busy for the moose. But in a small animal park near Levi, they were suddenly standing in the forest, looking friendly at the visitors. In Finland, of course, there are also many moose.

The next morning, it is the 9th of August, the weather has calmed down. The visibility is excellent, the wind is stable. So we leave Varjakka very carefully because the harbour entrance is shallow. Outside there is some swell waiting for us. It has been blowing all night. We pass the second shallow passage cautiously again, but there is no grounding this time. We are free to sail along the coast south of Oulu. We have 33 nautical miles to go to the pretty town of Raahe, which are completed in just under six hours. Between the skerries off Rahe, it gets calm, the islands cover the waves.

A pretty church with a cross shining golden in the sun welcomes the sailors on an offshore archipelago island. We moor again in the middle of town at the town quay, expecting it to be a little quieter here than in Oulu. This is true because, in Raahe, nothing is going on at all on this Monday evening. Is this the actual guest harbour, we ask ourselves? Because there is no infrastructure. But the location is excellent, on a long jetty with an outrigger. The Packing House museum is right next door. The town impresses with its wooden houses, just as the coastal handbook promised us. But at the same time, it seems strangely deserted. The guest harbour lies on the other side of the bay and shares its fate with one of Oulu's jetties: the way into town would simply be too far.

In the centre of Raahe, there is a bit more life. We visit a Mexican restaurant, which belongs to a Finnish chain and looks as if it could be anywhere in the world. Maybe the decoration with sombreros is a bit exaggerated after all. So we order a selection of enchiladas and quesadillas. The food is as good as a ready-made kitchen can deliver. Raahe, a small town with 25,000 inhabitants, puzzles the visitor. There is no other way to put it, the centre itself is ugly: where there are some shops, the houses have crumbling concrete facades. On the other hand, in the other part of Raahe, there are very well preserved historical buildings, between which not a soul can be seen. Here it's true: the streets with wooden houses are among the most beautiful and best-preserved that we have seen in Finland.

In the Pakkahuone Museum, which is the packing house, "Wanha Herra", the oldest diving suit in the world from the 18th century, is on display. The suit, made of leather with seams stuffed with pitch, looks incredible: There are discs for the eyes in the front, it was tied with a rope at the top, and a wooden tube could be used to pump in breathing air. A diver should be able to stay underwater for up to 40 minutes, as tests with a replica have recently shown. A remarkable piece from the beginnings of diving, presented in an excellent little museum in the north of Finland.

In Raahe, the Pakkahuone Museum is located directly in the harbour

9 THE COAST FROM RAAHE TO VAASA

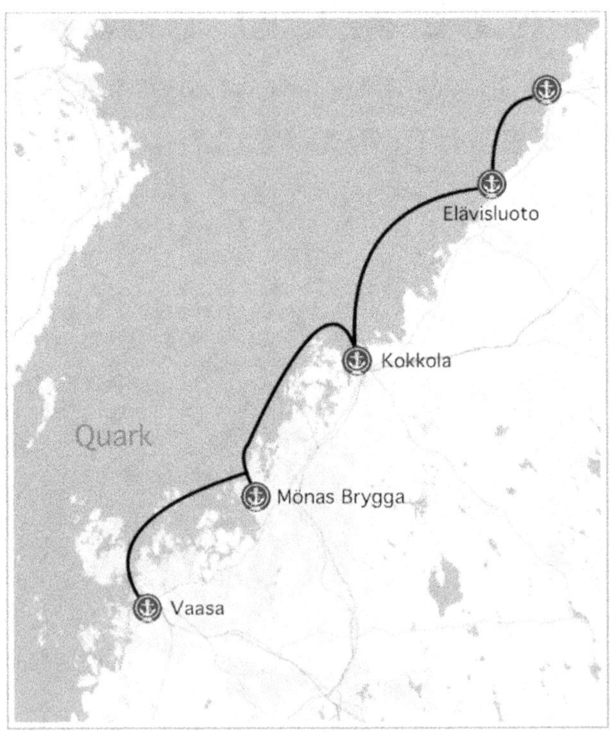

We are now facing a long, relatively straight stretch of coastline that unrolls southwest along the "Bay of Bothnia". It leads us again into the Quark at its southern end, this time on the Finnish side of the archipelago. The next bigger town is Kokkola. But we don't want to make the necessary 62 nautical miles straight off. After all, we came up here mainly to see a little of the northern part of the Bothnian Sea.

While studying the maps, several small harbours caught my eye. We get stuck for a while at the tiny village of Lankiperä. The nautical chart shows two small ports in the river's mouth, but they don't seem deep enough for sailing yachts. That's why we decide on Elävislouoto, which is 22 nautical miles south of Raahe. There it appears to be deep enough, and I set the course. Sailing southwest is lovely, but there is a stiff wind blowing again. Nevertheless, we take the mainsail and genoa in full size so that "Svanen" can make good speed. After 3 hours and 50 minutes, we take down the sails, motor around a headland and enter the small harbour.

Here again, there is enough space because Elävislouoto is a pure fishing harbour on a rather lonely coast. When ports are built and operated up here, they are only for fishermen. That does not exist at all at the German shores, inconceivable to hold out a port only for the fishery. But that seems to be normality up here.

We moor alongside a sizeable wooden jetty. Across the way, a friendly Finn is waving. He is tinkering with a small, about six meters long catamaran, which he has equipped with an electric drive. A true tinkerer's project: He has installed all kinds of electronics, but the vehicle does not look very seaworthy. That's why he doesn't want to go out with it in the windy weather today and instead retreats to the little house of the fishermen's cooperative. We take a walk into the woods behind the harbour. There, quite hidden between the trees, are some charming cottages with a view of the archipelago on the coast. At 19 degrees, the water is still relatively warm in the harbour of Elävislouoto, and because no ship comes, I go for a swim immediately in the harbour basin. Recreational skippers are left here free of charge, but there is no infrastructure. Never mind, the relaxed tranquillity of the small harbour captivates you.

The next day, another sailing centre on the Finnish coast should await us. The town of Kokkola has a friendly sailing club, which we reach after seven and a half hours. It was about 43 nautical miles there. A narrow channel leads to the sailing harbour, parallel to the industrial port, which disappears behind a long, drawn-out skerry. In Kokkola, children on optimists do a few laps around the harbour, and the club keeper welcomes us. He proudly shows us the new guest mooring, which has just been installed. So new that no other guest comes apart from us who could moor there.

From the locker, I rummage out one of our two onboard bikes, with which I want to cycle to the nearest supermarket. Unfortunately, the tires have hardly any pressure left. And because the tube of the folding bike has car valves, we also have no suitable air pump. We ask around in the whole sailing club, but nobody has a pump handy. I try my luck. Slowly I drive into the town on the no longer completely inflated tyre. It looks quite prosperous in its western suburb: Spacious houses have well-tended gardens. Because the garden fences are mostly missing, the place seems again very American.

The colossal supermarket a few kilometres away has every-thing your heart desires: Finnish meat, vegetables, bread, coffee and whatever else you need for food. There is also a small gas station, which unfortunately also has no compressed air. It doesn't help: I have to push the bike back with the purchases.

However, in the harbour, compensation for this bicycle trip is waiting for me: the most beautiful sauna of our journey so far. The sauna house was built behind the historic, large clubhouse.

It is already late evening, and it is getting dark. Just the right time for a sauna session. Through the windows of the wooden room, you can see the sun sinking over the Bothnian Sea. Then you open the outer door, and ten metres away, you can walk straight into the sea to recover from the heat of the sauna. Yes, that's it: The best sauna yet, at Kokkola Sailing Club.

This is the clubhouse of the Kokkola Sailing Club

On the way to Vaasa, we picked out another small, remote harbour: Mönas Brygga at a distance of 42 nautical miles. Beautiful weather with plenty of sunshine, but there is wind exactly from the southwest, from the front. We decide on a motor part. After all, after three days without shore power, the batteries could do with a bit of energy, and the diesel provides that. I would not be so relaxed about the motor trip if I knew that the south-westerly wind would last for days.

After the archipelago off Kokkola, we continue south until we finally drive up Mönassundet, where the small harbour is located. The way from Raahe to Vaasa is undoubtedly one of the most beautiful stretches of coast on this trip: It is quiet but not lonely, as there are still some sailboats on the way. Moreover, the coast is not entirely flat, but there are always hills and small skerries, the fairway is always deep enough.

On the way into the sound, you pass the small skerry Römsan, a large rock reaching into the fairway. It seems to literally float above the fairway. I have to make a detour around the granite boulder. With Brännskatagrundet, there is another harbour in the sound, but it does not look quite as idyllic as "Mönas Brygga", which lies a few miles further inland. There are also some army vehicles there. Uniformed men get out and set up camping chairs. They don't seem to be real soldiers, as they're pulling out fishing gear. Or are they?

Pretty fishermen's cabins in quiet Mönassund

We are already on the way to "Mönas Brygga". There are also several sailboats moored. There is a stone wall with an excellent bathing place next to the wide mooring bridge, where you can comfortably moor your boat at the front while a buoy holds the ship at the back. A group of older Finns sits at a table and plays cards at the edge. Indeed, the thermometer continues to show 19 degrees, so time for an extended bath in the Mönassund.

Because the wind is still blowing from the south, we must continue the trip under motor - or tick against the wind. I calculate the distance. 45.7 nautical miles to the next destination, to Vaasa, so a good stretch. Maybe it might be right again with the wind and the sail further out when we have left Mönassund? We set off around the peninsula of Digiberget in a wide arc and enter the archipelago fairway. The route we have chosen leads us close to many big and small islands. In addition, the sun shines from a cloudless sky. Besides the fairway, the sea here is less than one metre deep. You can safely forget about beating to the wind.

Instead, after a few hours, we head for a modern bridge, the Replot Bridge, which elegantly leads from the mainland to an offshore island. With its two supporting pillars, the roadway is suspended by wire ropes. It could be a copy of the Köhlbrand Bridge in Hamburg. However, with its clearance height of 24 metres, it is only half as high because ships with a height of 50 metres can pass at the Köhlbrand.

The Replot Bridge before Vaasa

Now it goes through small, narrow fairways closer and closer to Vaasa. Some sailors come towards us, who have set their spinnakers before the wind and pass quickly. After a few nautical miles, the shores move closer together, and we sail over a fairway towards the city. Everywhere there are villas on the banks. It reminds me of the Berlin Wannsee and the waterways in Spandau.

Most of the recreational harbours in Vaasa are located on the east side of the island of Vastklot, just opposite the city centre. The ferry from Umeå, which docks on the other side of the Quark in Sweden, also arrives at this island. There we moor at the very back, in the harbour of the "Segelförening". It is a friendly harbour, where almost only sailing yachts are moored. Even the harbour master has a boat, an Albin Vega, with which he makes a short trip before work and on which he also spends the night watch. He is very friendly and shows us the way.

By the way, Swedish is spoken in this club, as in some sailing clubs in Finland. In the meantime, there are more sailors in Finland than in the neighbouring country, as the harbour master explains to us.

"For many younger Swedes, sailing has become too cumbersome. They just want to get out on the water in a fast motorboat. It's still different here in Finland, even though we're also a bit lacking in new blood in the sailing clubs." At least that explains why we see more sailors again than on the opposite side of the Bothnian Sea. For example, the club has difficulty finding enough volunteers for harbour master duty. And because it is supposed to be manned at night, our harbour master has to work several nights in a row. He would like to sail more, as he tells us. But next week there is a trip with some clubmates.

The sauna in the harbour costs extra, 21 euros, but for that, there is a whole sauna hut located on the jetty and has a small terrace where you can recover from the really very hot sauna. We have quite a lot to do. Because on "Svanen", the lid of the cockpit locker is broken. Impressive for such thick teak wood. In addition, the water pump in the galley is damaged, and the foresail needs sewing. On the furling jib, there is weather protection made of UV-resistant fabric on the very outside, and this grey sheet is torn - in no less than 16 places, as I count. It's just as well that the sailcloth itself hasn't suffered any damage so far.

The friendly harbormaster drives up in his older Saab in true Scandinavian style the following day. His shift is over. A colleague has replaced him. Therefore, he can now drive with us to an outfitter, which is not within walking distance of the port. Before, he had still put the German flag on the flagpole next to the Finnish - we are the only sailors visiting from Germany in Vaasa, as he explains.

The outfitter is closed, so we continue to the next shop. There, at least, we get a sturdy board to support the locker lid, boat paint, and a foot pump for the galley, which seems to be one-to-one with the model onboard. I still had electric pumps on the previous boat, but "Svanen" was equipped with foot pumps for drinking water, which I have really come to appreciate. You can dose the water nicely with one foot as it flows out of the tap, and electricity is not needed for this. So I am happy about the replacement pump, including mounting hardware.

Only tape to patch the tears in the weather protection of the furling jib is not available. We still have some yellow tape on board specifically for mending sails. But it would have to be sewn on. We can cover it with silver tape so that it doesn't stand out so much, and we don't have 16 yellow stripes in the jib. In the afternoon, Birgit wants to try out the sewing machine of the sailing club, a big, ancient model with pedal drive. But we can't find out how it works, and the club members shrug their shoulders: nobody knows how to operate the old sewing machine. So we glue the repair strips onto the sail. First yellow, then silver-grey, that could last a while.

Now we are going on a memorable shopping trip: We drive to the Iittala Outlet Vaasa, which is located behind the city centre in a shopping centre. We cover the way with two "Tier"-scooters, known from Hamburg or Berlin, quite quickly. There are actually reasonable offers of the household goods brand from Finland in the Outlet. A set "Mainio" is partly discounted. We take it. But we need it incredibly sturdily packed, we explain to the lady at the checkout because we are on our way to Germany by sailboat. On the way back we take a taxi. The dishes are stowed under the forward berth, carefully padded with cushions - may they survive the storms that still lie ahead of us.

The German flag is also flown in the "Vaasa Segelförening"

Vaasa is located on a peninsula, on which again a rectangular road network was built. The university town has around 67,000 inhabitants, but its tall houses make it seem larger. Vaasa is one of the centres of the Swedish-speaking minority in Finland: after all, a quarter of the inhabitants speak Swedish. The city centre starts when you pass the big "Vaasan Kirkko", the brick church, from the harbour. The pretty market hall, "Vaasan Kauppahalli", is a few blocks to the east. There is only one catch to the hall: the lovely shops, the food stalls and the nice café at the end close already at 5 pm.

Then life on the Hovioikeudenpuistikko is far from over. In this nightlife district, where several bars and pubs are lined up next to each other, the bars don't open until late. But there is also something going on near the harbour, on the "Inre Hamnen Terrace", which is just opposite "Svanen". In front of the terrace there are a lot of deck chairs on the lawn and on the quay. In the restaurant, you can eat well and also drink. Until 6 pm there is a happy hour where the glass of beer costs only four euros, later in the evening the price climbs to six euros - for 0,33 cl, mind you. In summer, even in Corona times, regular live concerts fill the harbour basin with sound. Above it all towers the stand of a high-voltage line that runs across the harbour basin and was renewed a few years ago. Before, the line too close to the shore was a problem for some tall sailboats. But the new line is very high, and the mast is illuminated at night in bright colours.

INFO: IN THE GALLEY

We can prepare a lot in the galley. There is hardly anything more excellent than to brighten up a sailing trip in cool weather with a cup of hot coffee (or maybe tea for the British?). Or cooking an authentic meal on two flames. But even if you just like to drink tea, the question is: How do I get the water hot? Your ship's batteries are not a choice for this. Any hot water heater would eat up too much electricity. An electric kettle might serve well if the ship is in port and you have shore power. Some yachts already have microwaves on board. But it gets more exciting at sea when there is no more power connection.

You can use a gas stove that is connected to a gas bottle. This is the standard on new yachts. A gas stove will be installed if you order a new large series yacht. The disadvantage is that the gas bottle must be housed separately on the boat with a vent, and the gas system must be serviced and checked regularly, at least in Germany. A safer option is a kerosene stove, the standard on yachts for decades. We also have a Swedish Optimus model 154 on "Svanen", which is gimballed and nicely integrated into the galley by the shipyard.

Unfortunately, this burner is not very easy to operate: You have to build up the pressure with a hand pump, then pour a shot glass full of spirit into the burner pot and light it. It takes a minute or so for the actual burner to heat up enough for you to turn on the regulator and for the kerosene to come out in gaseous form and burn. If the burner isn't hot enough, there may be sizable pilot flames, which have also sooted the ceiling above the pantry for us on occasion. However, if everything is running correctly, you'll have a nice hot flame that's good for cooking on two flames. The Swedish Optimus burners are no longer manufactured, but there is still the (quite expensive) British series of the manufacturer Taylor's available.

Cleaner and less complicated is a spirit burner, which, however, does not develop the heat of a kerosene burner. And then there are the diesel stoves, such as those offered by the Finnish company Wallas. Their disadvantage: they take a long time to get hot. The advantage is that you bring the fuel with you when you connect the stove to the ship's diesel tank. If we just want to have a quick coffee, we use a gas stove with cartridges. The small cartridges are individually not as dangerous as a whole gas system, they burn cleanly, and the kettle gets hot very quickly.

There are no special requirements for the cookware. You can take the pots, kettles and pans that you are comfortable with at home. A thick bottom is quite helpful because the kerosene burner gets very hot. It is beneficial to have intense LED lighting in the pantry. Not only are these lights bright, but they are also power-efficient, and a well-lit countertop is really a lot of fun. On older ships, you will often find fluorescent tubes in the galley.

By the way, as a coffee fan, I tried out a whole range of systems. 12-volt devices used in the car were among them as well as a capsule coffee machine for shore power or a rarer capsule machine with a hand pump from the US. My conclusion: all this is not worth the effort. The simplest method on board is still the hand filter filled with coffee powder on a thermos. With the kettle, which has a thermometer, I can make very aromatic coffee quickly and cheaply - so good that I also filter by hand at home. Incidentally, I also tried the spare petroleum stove we still have at home in the kitchen. It worked. However, unlike the coffee filter, this stove has not caught on in-home use.

Mr. Moose says: *It is excellent what effort you humans make to prepare your food. We moose are vegetarians, and we don't eat every-thing we find in nature. We depend on nitrogenous, energy- and protein-rich, fine-fibre food. That's why we look for the tastiest food on deciduous trees and other plants and like to nibble on buds and shoots of woody plants. We also have a pretty big lower lip for that. Now, if you absolutely must heat your food, look for a safe method, preferably without gas. I don't want to see your boat go up in flames.*

10 STORM IN REPOSAARI

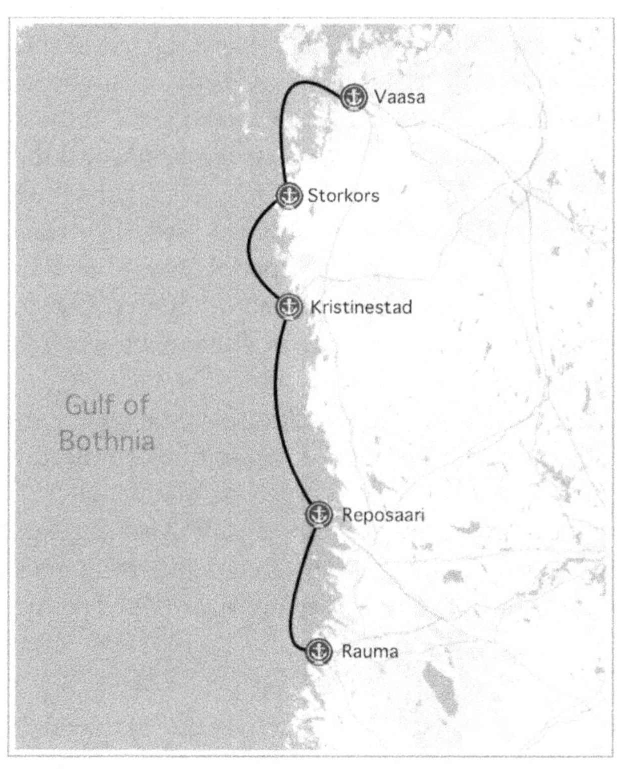

After a few days, it was time to leave Vaasa and move further south. Again we could sail through the archipelago of the Quark, which stretches in front of Vaasa. There are many more small islands on the Finnish side than on the Swedish side. And again, the islands were built up with tiny holiday houses. There was also a charming harbour among them, which we left on the port side. We had chosen a small fishing harbour on the map as a destination. We knew roughly what to expect, and so it came: A beautiful, secluded port, in which some fishing boats had moored, but without any infrastructure.

After 35 nautical miles, we entered Storkors. With 2.50 meters of water depth, there were no problems with our boat. Unfortunately, there was once again no water and the use of the cottage, which claimed to be a "dry toilet", can only be discouraged. But there were no mosquitoes. We had moored right at the end of the pier, which jutted far out into the harbour basin, and the pests couldn't find their way there. A sailor's adage runs through my head: if the wind is blowing towards the land, this would attract the mosquitoes, as the smell of the people would be transmitted. Fortunately, in Storkors this makes no difference. Leaving the harbour, we follow the same narrow channel between the skerries we had entered.

Kristinestad is the next destination. On the way there, we moor in Kaskinen, a pretty little town with a commercial harbour and which lies between two archipelago islands. There Birgit picked up lunch from a nearby restaurant. Also, an excellent way to travel: Just stop for lunch. You can quickly drive in from the northwest to Kaskinen and out again towards the southwest.

A fountain in Kristinestad harbour

Kristinestad lies at the end of a small fjord. The city already announced itself by the increasing development on the shore in front of the port. In the "Hotel Kristina", we check-in for the guest harbour, and the operator is a friendly Finn.

"You're from Germany, with the sailboat? I think that's great," he says. "We went to Travemünde a lot with the Finnjet. Always with our motorcycles. But today, we don't do that so much anymore." At this, he waves to his wife, with whom he runs the hotel. Apparently, he no longer has the time for long motorcycle tours. "You guys need to use the sauna quickly now, though," he tells us. "There is a group coming later. They have reserved the facility." And so, the friendly hotel owner practically "urges" us to visit the sauna.

Next to the hotel is a huge supermarket where you can perfectly stock up on food. From the boat you have a beautiful view of the city in the evening, in front of which an illuminated water fountain shoots up into the air.

After many days with unfavourable wind directions, it now turns to the northeast. The wind is still weak initially, but then it increases the next day significantly. These are just the right conditions for our long beat to Reposaari, 48 nautical miles away. As we approach Reposaari, it has already freshened up quite a bit. I've seldom experienced such timing: we've just decided to take down the sails because we're about to enter the harbour, then they're down and lashed, and already a thunderstorm squall with dense showers is hitting. Regardless of the rain, two dinghy sailors cross in the entrance, which I find pretty brave.

Just in time, the Finnish Meteorological Institute has issued a wind and wave warning for the next day. It is supposed to blow with wind force seven, which is "dangerous for smaller boats", as it says in the warning message. Soaking wet, we push ourselves into the well-protected berth. The next day we can't think of going any further. The boat sways so much at the jetty that I feel a bit queasy. In the harbour snack bar, there is fast food, which was not defrosted very well. In general, the harbour of Reposaari is no highlight. We lie in front of a sign that advertises the not exactly cheap harbour fees in big letters and clarifies that there is no discount for several days if one has not announced this on arrival. Already the use of the laundry room cost eight Euros. If you now add the condition of the not quite clean sanitary facilities, the price is clearly excessive.

The next day the wind is still blowing hard. We still want to try it and cast off. No sooner have we left the marina than a steep swell comes up in the harbour entrance. The waves, which didn't look so wild from the shore, are now piling up in front of us. I guess the water walls are two metres high, and "Svanen" is bravely digging into them. Of course, this is too much for safe sailing. In a wave trough, I turn the ship around, no problem, and after four nautical miles, we run into Reposaari again and moor in the same place as before.

"Svanen" is safely moored, and the harbour master collects the money again. Afterwards, we go into the village and visit the "Holy Smoke" restaurant on the water. It must be a hip address because it is full of locals. The food is indeed quite good and is served on original wooden boards.

It should be as windy as on Wednesday also on Thursday. Nevertheless, we want to dare the same manoeuvre again the next day. We sail out of the marina, approach the industrial harbour and the wide harbour exit. What a nasty surprise: The waves are even higher today than yesterday. Unprotected, the Bothnian Sea rushes directly towards the entrance of Reposaari. The waves follow each other very quickly and are incredibly steep. When "Svanen" is in a wave trough, you can see the next wave rushing diagonally above you. Also, the navigation on the tablet is broken again, the screen flickers. We turn around again and disappear behind the thick breakwater that offers protection. This time, however, we are no longer heading to port to the guest harbour of Reposaari but to starboard to the Mäntyluoto sailing club, which is only a few nautical miles away.

"That looked terrible. We watched your journey from the shore," says a Finnish sailor standing on the shore with his wife. "Yes," she agrees. "In the troughs of the waves, your boat was no longer visible. Only the tip of the mast was still sticking out. We called the harbormaster as soon as you turned around." We had met these two in a couple of ports before. And now that was a friendly move, so the harbour master knew that another boat was about to come. With the help of the two Swedes, we moor safely in strong winds. This harbour is more unprotected than the guest harbour. We stop next to a Vindö 40. This interestingly has precisely the same Seldén rig as our Vindö 32. The harbour master comes and has a chat. "Either you donate something to our harbour, or you don't pay anything," he explains the somewhat strange system. "If you donate, then please only ten euros." Of course, we're happy to donate that as it's dirt cheap for Scandinavia. He seems to enjoy walking around in the wind and weather and taking care of the jetties.

The cockpit tent protects against rain

The clubhouse of the sailing club is now at our disposal. Inside there is a high-tech sauna, whose stove is embedded in the bench and has a lid to close. Unfortunately, it doesn't get really hot. I can't cope with the control panel with digital display, the operation of which is simply illogical. So the sauna is cancelled, but the shower is hot. From the shore, you can see out to the open sea. And now, standing safely on the rocks, it actually looks even more threatening than it did from onboard. The waves roar in with foamy crests and crash onto the rocks, splashing their spray for metres. I can't believe that we wanted to go through there just now. In contrast, it's nice to see how safe and pleasant you can stay in a friendly Finnish sailing club.

One day later, we can continue our journey. That is unexpectedly difficult. There is still a strong swell in front of Reposaari. We have to go through it now. At least the waves are not as high as in the three days before. We want to make progress now, as the distance ahead of us is still long. But a group of archipelagos a few nautical miles away shields the route from the open sea, which should make for calmer waters.

Once again, it must be the third failure, the Raymarine autopilot stops working. And once again, I hook up the "old-timer" to take some of the steering off our hands from the hours of cruising. Today the old autopilot is in shape, keeping a straight course. It manages quite well in these conditions. The wind is blowing sideways at about five Beaufort, which seems to suit the ship as well as the device.

There are calm conditions within the archipelago, and a sailing club holds a regatta there. The yachts sail spinnaker before the wind and glide through the calm water. But behind the next skerry we leave the sheltered area and head for the open sea. Here a strong wave comes from the side. Furthermore, it starts to rain.

There are two routes to choose from: behind the island of Aikonmaa or around it. In this weather and the poor visibility, I prefer to go around. True to the motto, there is at least enough space. Besides, power lines run across the bay and I'm not sure if the clearance would be sufficient for our yacht. The way around the outside of the island is a detour, but it seems to me to be the safe way.

Seen from the shore: The sea is rough off Reposaari

We are now sailing very close to the Olkiluoto nuclear power plant. Since the end of the seventies, two reactors have been in operation here, each producing over 800 megawatts. Next to it is the construction site of section 3: it is to be one of the most powerful in the world and will eventually generate 1600 megawatts of electricity. The work, seen as Finland's clear commitment to nuclear energy, has been underway since 2005 but has been delayed repeatedly. Due to the rain, not much of the plant is visible, and we are glad when we finally reach the approach buoy for Rauma and can turn back to the archipelago. With the waves we run behind the islands in front of the harbour.

Suddenly, it is quiet off the industrial harbour. Only the wind whistles through the rigging. We take down the sails, look around and head to starboard, where there is supposed to be a small harbour behind the cargo quays. That was exactly the wrong decision, as it would turn out a little later. But hadn't the coastal handbook also shown an illustration with a clear arrow pointing the way to the harbour? And isn't this jetty also shown on the nautical chart?

We chug along with the cargo ships and pass a shipyard where the new building for the ferry from Vaasa to Umeå is under construction, an elegantly curved ferry powered by LNG, which will be somewhat cleaner than conventional diesel.

But what we are heading for now is not the harbour for pleasure boats. That is on the other side of the peninsula with the industrial harbour. Instead, we drive again into a small fishing port. A rough facility where some boats are moored. At least there is also a police station at the harbour. The officers don't seem to mind that we moor at the fishing pier for once. And also, a Finn, who controls the lines at his working boat, explains to us that we can stay here quietly until tomorrow. So we are allowed to stay. And what more do you want? We lie safely moored behind the concrete pier with strong wind and rain. There is even electricity to charge the batteries.

Unfortunately, we don't get to see much of Rauma itself. The town with almost 40,000 inhabitants is supposed to be quite pretty, but the city centre is a good walk away from our industrial harbour. At the same time, the hard day's sailing wears on the bones. You can't have everything.

The following day Birgit notices a man taking pictures of us and our sailboat from his car. He quickly rolls up the window when she speaks to him and speeds away. I already thought of an "undercover" investigator of the Rauma police. But we don't see what this action was all about until a few days later, by chance, on the Internet. The man was a "ship spotter", that is, a ship lover. He apparently likes to take pictures of ships, especially those moored in Rauma harbour, which he then photographs and logs. And the sailing yacht with the German flag at the stern in the fishing harbour just made him curious. He uploaded the pictures of "Svanen" on "Marinetraffic" and linked them with our ship. If you query our AIS position there, you will see the photos of this ship lover who, by the way, has already posted hundreds of ships there.

Actually a good idea, I think, because a photo of our ship was still missing at "Marinetraffic". Now we are in the company of large tankers, fancy cruise ships and luxury yachts. Therefore, I thank you very much - also to the next "Shipspotter", who should photograph us a little later.

Our AIS transmitter, which I would not want to do without, especially in poor visibility, continuously transmits the international identification number "MMSI" when we are underway. Plus the course and speed. And that just arouses curiosity, especially in international waters where not so many German boats arrive.

INFO: A YACHT IS NOT A DINGHY

As you know, a dinghy can capsize, but not a keelboat (unless a huge wave knocks it over). As my sailing instructor once said, the keelboat's mast is more likely to break than to tip over from the wind pressure. But it is not only stability that dinghies and yachts differ in. You also have to handle the keelboat a little differently, for example, when setting or recovering the sails or when reefing. On a classic "slup", i.e. a yacht with a mast as well as a foresail and mainsail, you will be sailing with a working jib, a large genoa or possibly a small storm sail, in addition to your mainsail. And those have to be set first.

You probably still know the sailing school wisdom that you should go into the wind when setting the sails. However, this basic rule only applies to a limited extent when you are underway with your yacht. Indeed, it is easier and more gentle on the material to set the mainsail into the wind. But it is not safer: especially strong wind and high waves can make it dangerous to stay on the forecastle when you go into the wind. Besides, the boat will then only make speed under the engine. If all halyards on your yacht should be redirected to the cockpit, you do not necessarily have to go to the mast to set the sails - unless you have to untie the sails, for example, from the boom, or a part like a sail batten gets caught when you hoist the sails.

Another option would be to go on a downwind course. Downwind, the apparent wind speed on the deck of your boat decreases as you are sailing "with the wind". Also, the wave action is much less than if you were going directly into the wind. You can also set or lower the mainsail on a downwind course - we have tried this manoeuvre often enough on "Svanen", and I promise: it is safer than working on the mast when there are dangerous wave movements in the wind. However, the load on the sail is higher should it rub on the shrouds.

It is also easier to set, reef or furl the jib or genoa if you are downwind and the mainsail is on the same side as the headsail. Then the lee of the mainsail covers the jib or genoa, and you can work on it more easily.

But there is another way: you take a course of about 60 to 70 degrees to the wind, so a moderate upwind course. If your headsail is already up or still up, it can drive the boat further. You can then open the boom so that the mainsail is precisely in the wind. In a way, it combines several advantages: The yacht continues to make speed, but you no longer have wind pressure in the mainsail. A dangerous disadvantage: the boom could swing back and forth if it cannot be secured with a line to the front. In practice, try all the possibilities, including reefing the sails. Reducing or increasing sail area is also extremely important at sea. However, the stubborn "into the wind" rule alone will not get you everywhere.

Mr. Moose says: Up and down, again and again. If there's anything we moose don't like, it's these waves. They also shake your boats quite a bit. It's good that there are so many small islands up here in my home country. You can always hide behind the archipelago to make your manoeuvres. I watch you do it.

11 THROUGH THE ARCHIPELAGO TO ÅLAND

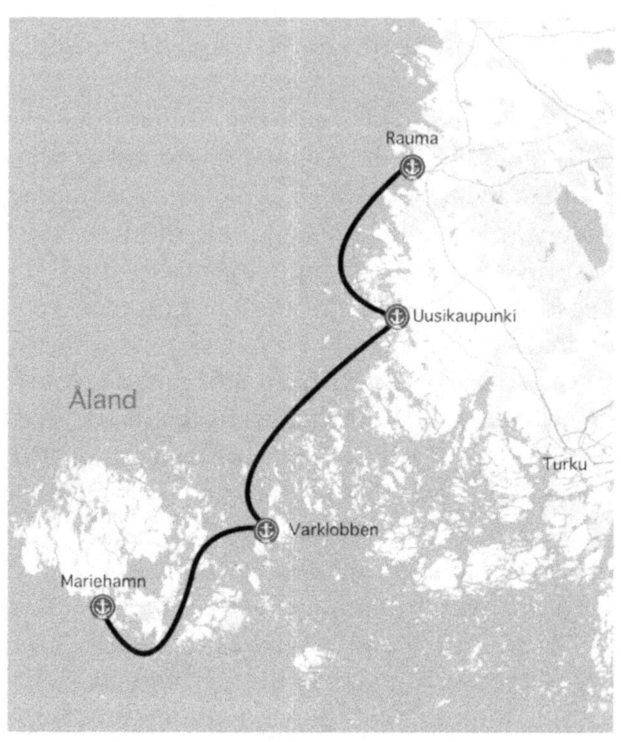

Once again, I think a "real" port is needed, one with all the comforts. Already in Reposaari, the sanitary facilities were closed in the morning and in the industrial harbour of Rauma there were none at all. A nice bath in the harbour basin was really out of the question. I studied the nautical charts. Again, the coastal handbook is no great help, as there are gaps in the port descriptions. So I compare the "Open CPN"-Finland nautical chart with the Navionics nautical chart and then check against the satellite images from Google Maps. This has given us many an exciting fishing port. And even though our next destination, the little town with the funny name of Uusikaupunki, is already a bit better known, I prefer to check the entrance to the harbour by satellite photo. After all, we don't want to head for an industrial harbour again instead of the harbour for pleasure boats.

The day had started with a surprise. Towards morning there was a small bang, followed by a low hiss from the cockpit. I struggled out of the forward berth, unlocked the door and saw: the automatic lifejacket had inflated itself and was now lying under the sprayhood. I had thought this was a good place to store the vest yesterday. There it should be protected and still well ventilated.

But the rain came obliquely from the rear and somehow dissolved the small salt tablet that keeps the cartridge closed. The bang was - logically, the opening of the vest. Intrigued, I look at the thick yellow something inflated under the sprayhood. It seems to be a nice, solid material. Well, the vest had to be serviced in the winter anyway, and we still have two vests, so we can probably get over the failure of a vest without having to make any sacrifices in safety. So off we go, "Svanen" chugs out of the industrial harbour, turns onto the nice wide fairway to port, and we set sail. With 18 knots of wind, the Vindö ploughs through the water off the archipelago of Rauma. It didn't feel at all like a strong breeze was blowing, as the islands take the edge off the wind and waves. And the route we are following also fits very well. But slowly, the archipelago becomes sparser again as we head south, and decent waves come at us from the sea. The wind increases to 24 knots. The little old-timer autopilot is still doing its job onboard. It manages to keep the ship on course to some extent. But soon, I will have to take the original autopilot apart correctly to find the actual fault.

Finally, we sail again in a fairway that runs narrowly between the skerries. After a few bends, the small town of Uusikaupunki comes into view. Again we are greeted by an industrial harbour where some roll-on roll-off freighters are moored. But don't worry, I tell myself, this time the route is carefully planned. "Svanen" makes a tack to starboard, a turn to port, and we are already in the approach to the extensive leisure harbour. After 32 nautical miles from Rauma, we moor directly at the guest harbour, situated in front of a granary. Beautiful flowers are planted on the shore, on the other side of the port is a tennis court, which is well attended.

The amenities of a well-maintained Scandinavian guest harbour lie before us. A handful of boats are also moored here. There is a café, a restaurant, the sanitary facilities and of course in Finland also a sauna, which was nicely built into a wooden cottage. We eat in the nice pizzeria at the port, where the beer "Lapin Kulta" is reasonably priced.

Then I'll take care of the autopilot. The piece is three years old and was not quite cheap. Besides, it should be much more robust in type than its "old-timer" cousin. After a lot of screwing, Birgit finds a cable on the back of the small motor that drives the arm that moves the tiller. If you push the cable down, the pilot doesn't work anymore.

Evening atmosphere in the harbour of Uusikaupunki

Clear case: It needs to be soldered. For just such cases, I carry a small soldering set on board. And even though I'm not an electrical specialist: In the light of the bright lamp above our salon table, I make the connection bombproof, I hope. The arm moves with a cheerful "Sirr", "Sirr" when I press the appropriate buttons on the control box. The sea can come.

Meanwhile, it got dark in Uusikaupunki at 9.30 pm. The bright nights are now, in the second half of August, already over. Besides, we are quite a bit further south. But the lighting in the harbour looks nice: Lamps are fixed under the planks at the jetties, illuminating the shore and the water. They give a certain elegance to the place. A local artist displays his work on a handsome wooden two-master moored in front of the café. These are all ornate lighthouses that shine in the nightfall. Uusikaupunki has a certain charm. At the salon table, we plan and calculate. In front of us are the nautical charts. On the laptop shines the electronic map. There are only about 50 nautical miles left from Uusikaupunki to Turku. The city with almost 200,000 inhabitants and its large harbour would be a good destination on the way south.

On the other hand, the weather forecast announces terrible conditions. The weather is supposed to hold about two days, but then it should worsen according to the forecast, with winds up to 30 knots, i.e. seven Beaufort, to be expected. And this is supposed to continue for a few days. What's more, it's already 23 August. In September, I want to be on my way back to Germany and no longer sail up here in the Finnish archipelago - a good decision, as it should turn out.

So we decide to leave Turku on the port side and set course for the Åland Islands. Now I prefer to have a time buffer for the way back. And just like Helsinki, Turku also offers itself for a later trip. So now we are sailing in the archipelago between Finland and the Åland Islands. We are on our way to the small harbour of Varklobben on the island of Kumlinge, a day trip of 42 nautical miles.

It's nice that the newer autopilot steers perfectly again. But whoops, what kind of wind is it today, I ask myself. The storm is not supposed to arrive for another two days. A gust pushed "Svanen" firmly to one side, and we had already set the first reef. The route leads us along the open sea, passing the archipelago in the north. It doesn't help. We have to reef further. Fortunately, the next archipelago is not far for this purpose. This is an advantage when sailing along the edge of the archipelago: You can quickly "slip away" behind a skerry.

But even there, the bow rises and falls strongly. Birgit is at the mast, hooked with the safety belt, while I steer the boat slowly but steadily towards the beach of the skerry. The reefing with the ribbons is really awkward. The Vindö 32 with her "Seldén rig" actually had a so-called single-line reefing system, but it has not been used for years. There are no more lines in the boom. "I'll have to fix that in the winter," I take it upon myself. With a dedicated winch on the mast, the reefing could be safely brought in. So all that remains is to wait for my wife to do the complicated work on the mast on the swaying forecastle. I make sure that the boat does not run off course.

We move between the archipelago after half of the trip, where it becomes calmer. We pass a narrow passage then it goes next to larger islands to the south. And finally, we "turn" onto the approach to the harbour. We take down the sails again in the shelter of the opposite archipelago, sail in and moor "Svanen": aft the stern buoy, forward two lines to the jetty. Done, with a good wind.

The harbour is charming: the jetties consist of wooden bridges anchored in the rocks of the archipelago and lead to the shore. There is the harbour master's cottage and, as usual, a sauna house. Unfortunately, the café, which belongs to the harbour, is already closed. Apart from us, there is only one other boat in the sanctuary. It is a German who is touring the Åland Islands with his wife. On the jetty, he tells me how comfortable his boat is, how wide the berths are, and that he has a three-line reefing system.

I am friendly and agree that his ship is really well equipped.

But in retrospect, I have to smile a bit. What do wide berths and his reefing system really do for him? Does he really have a perfectly equipped ship? What matters is seaworthiness, after all. I would always choose the less well-equipped but more seaworthy ship and the more exciting trip. Although Svanen is not badly equipped. The Vindö is exceptionally seaworthy. Only the triple reefing system, I would also quite like to have that on the mast. But the equipment is there. It just needs to be "revived".

Svanen has moored at the pretty jetty at Varklobben

The weather apparently wants to give us some breathing space before the storm approaches, as I discover in the evening when studying the forecasts. Tomorrow is not supposed to be so windy yet. The five models that "Predictwind" shows for this sea area agree on that. The Finnish Meteorological Institute has not yet issued a wind warning for tomorrow, but they have for the day after tomorrow. We want to go to Mariehamn. Secretly, I'm thinking of taking a ferry from the capital of the Åland Islands to get to Turku regardless of the storm. Because they constantly shuttle between Sweden and Finland and call at Mariehamn to allow duty-free sales - a unique feature that the EU has allowed the islands. Only it's not like on the German island of Helgoland - you can't shop duty-free in Mariehamn itself.

Mariehamn can be approached from three directions: The recommended routes for pleasure boats lead to the West Harbour from the south and the west. From the east, the course goes to the east harbour of Mariehamn and passes a small channel with a bascule bridge. To be on the safe side, I first mark out both routes, while outside, the moon is rising and bathes the beautiful archipelago harbour with its two boats in a cold, white light.

But to change from the east to the west harbour is not so easy, because you would have to make a big bow around the island Jarsö with the boat. That would be precisely 14.7 nautical miles. Therefore, we decide to go straight to the west harbour. We want to go on to Sweden later on, and this could be a long beat. If we start from the west harbour, it would be noticeably shorter.

We have a moderate breeze, leave the small harbour, set the mainsail, unfurl the genoa, and sail through the archipelago in bright sunshine. The tablet in the cockpit shows us the route, a clear line on the electronic sea chart, which we follow. It goes close to Vardö along. But all of a sudden, I'm stunned: Why do we keep heading west instead of southwest? Suddenly, I realize that we are on the direct way to the eastern harbour. These are the pitfalls of electronic navigation: I had simply loaded the wrong route and stubbornly followed it. A screen like this always only shows a section when it is enlarged. But that's not a big deal: we've already sailed a few nautical miles around the route, but with the nice wind and the sun it's not so bad. Birgit takes the tiller while I mark out a new path with the tablet, which leads us back to the direct route to the west harbour.

Before the harbour of Långnäs, the ferries come towards us. The fairway from Stockholm to Turku leads here in some bends directly through the archipelago. But the big ships are not disturbing. It is always fascinating to see such a colossus coming up behind an archipelago, turning, coming straight towards it and then heading for the harbour of Långnäs or driving on. But nevertheless, I am glad to turn to starboard and take a smaller fairway while the Finnlines, the Viking-Line and the Silja-Line stay behind us. But there is traffic here too. A smaller ferry shuttling between the islands of the archipelago comes rushing up.

Of course, we make room for it and the captain waves friendly from his wheelhouse.

Then something happens that I hadn't expected: the wind goes to sleep. The forecast had already indicated that it would become less in the afternoon, but not that we would have no wind at all between the archipelago. "Svanen" is bobbing in front of a small forest on the rocky coast. Just now, we were making four knots, now only one. It doesn't help: We take down the sails, the Volvo Penta has to take over and bring us the remaining three hours to Mariehamn.

We drive through the suburbs, approaching the capital of the Åland Islands from the south. Already from a distance, we can see the "Pommern", the impressive four-master, which is moored in the western harbour of Mariehamn and can be visited. And also, a ferry of the Viking-Line wants to call at the port. Fortunately, the two fairways are still separated before they meet: our small one and the big one for the ferries. Then we pass the ferry harbour and head for the sailing club of Mariehamn with its beautiful wooden clubhouse. Also, here in the guest harbour, there is not much going on. We "grab" the stern buoy with the hook again and go to the jetty to moor. But this time, I double the lines in front - because the storm, which is not noticeable yet, is coming closer according to the forecast.

INFO: THE INDISPENSABLE MARINE RADIO

Sometimes I looked a bit sadly at our grey box on the card table: "What are you actually good for, except for emergencies?" I wanted to ask the device. But that's precisely the point: to establish a connection in an emergency. Because unlike mobile phones, we have a range of about 30 nautical miles with it - the marine radio antenna is mounted at the top of the mast. The mobile phone networks only reach a few nautical miles out to sea and in Finland a little further. Another advantage is: With the radio, all ships and boats in the vicinity can listen in, for example on emergency channel 16.

And in contrast to a distress beacon, an "EPIRB", which can automatically send out a distress signal, you can talk to the rescue control centre using the radio. This can be very helpful, especially in a dicey situation. The control centre can ask you important questions and give you instructions.

The radio also allows you to talk to ships in the vicinity. You can ask a commercial vessel coming towards you for its course or even for weather information. This would be virtually impossible with a cell phone and much more cumbersome with a satellite phone. Some harbours, bridges and locks can also be easily radioed. If you are sailing in German waters in the North and Baltic Seas, it is also a good idea to subscribe to "Delta Papa 07", which operates the remaining German coastal radio stations. There are other weather services on the marine radio in other parts of Europe.

New radios all have DSC technology built-in, which allows you to radio ships by entering their number (the MMSI). With "Svanen" we took over a great old "Sailor" radio with a black telephone handset. Unfortunately, that was no longer registrable, so I had to replace it with said gray box. The new radios must also have a GPS receiver built-in so that in an emergency, the position is automatically transmitted. A little reminder on the side: GPS is not a gimmick in such emergencies, it is very important! So: A GPS belongs on every radio if it is not already built-in.

Finally, you can enjoy some maritime entertainment if you leave the radio running (which, incidentally, you are obliged to do if it is permanently installed onboard). For example, off the south coast of Sweden, the Coast Guard was scouting for polluters. I was able to overhear the conversation between a Coast Guard employee and a somewhat huffy radio officer aboard a Russian freighter. "You just left an oil trail behind you. Did you discharge anything into the water?" the Coast Guard asked. No, denied the radio operator. He had done nothing at all and knew of nothing. "Yes, you did. We were watching you do it. In fact, we are right on top of you," returned the Coast Guard, which was on a reconnaissance plane. The captain was informed that a detailed investigation was coming his way.

Mr. Moose says: *You've come up with something: Radios with which you can contact other sailors even though you can't see them. Of course, the best thing is to avoid dangerous situations in the first place. We moose prefer to wait a little and not go into stormy waters. And you should only make an emergency call if there is an emergency. After all, you go into a lot of trouble when you receive an emergency call. The rescue chain of the entire coast is then activated.*

12 MARIEHAMN, THE CAPITAL OF THE ÅLAND ISLANDS

The rain slaps against the deckhouse windows, the wind howls in the shrouds. The next day, the storm came as predicted. But "Svanen" lies safely moored in the sailing harbour ÅSS in the western port of Mariehamn. Around us, out of the open bulkhead, I can see the "Pavilion", the sailing club's restaurant with its imaginative wooden structure with richly decorated beams. It is a mixture of Nordic and Far Eastern architecture. Directly in front of "Svanen" lies the "Pommern", behind it the cruise ship "Birka". That has become a victim of the pandemic: The shipping company, which belonged to a smaller ferry line, had organized short cruises from Stockholm to Mariehamn with the steamer. When the first wave of covid hit, the cruises between Sweden and Finland were cancelled. The shipping company is no longer in business, and the beautiful ship lies on the quay until it finds a buyer.

An actual monument is the "Pommern", the third "Flying-P-Liner" I get to see. There is the "Passat" in Travemünde in Germany, moored at a jetty on the Priwall. There is the "Peking", which was moored for many years at the South Street Seaport in New York before the plan was implemented to bring her back to

Hamburg. She has undergone a significant refurbishment and is now moored in the Hansa Harbour in Hamburg, somewhat hidden away by the Harbour Museum. And there is her sister ship "Pommern", moored in Mariehamn. No fewer than twelve of these four- and five-masted steel barques were launched between 1892 and 1924 for the Hamburg shipping company F. Laeisz.

The "Pommern" in the western harbour of Mariehamn

They are said to have been renowned for their robustness and speed, and for their safety - which is unlikely to apply to the disastrous sinking of the "Pamir" in 1957. But now we have the "Pommern" lying directly in front of our bow, which had been commissioned in May 1903. Twenty years later, the Finnish shipowner Gustaf Erikson had bought the "Pommern" and stationed it in its new homeport of Mariehamn. Instead of salt-petre from Chile, she transported wheat between Australia and

Europe. In 1945 she returned to her home country with a cargo of grain, which was her last commercial voyage for Erikson. In 1953, the family donated the ship to the town of Mariehamn. Today she is integrated into the town's very worth seeing maritime museum and has been given her own dock. You can walk on it and take a look at the ship from all sides.

The stormy, rainy day was just the right time to visit the museum and the "Pommern". It is impressive to see how the crew worked and lived on the ship. So everything took place on deck and in the superstructures, below are simply holds.

You could get from the crew's quarters to the helm or officers' mess through the heavy rain. There were also chambers for a handful of passengers at the stern of the barque. With their wooden panelling, they look really luxurious - especially if you've visited the crew's sleeping quarters before. An excellent audio explanation runs from the headphones you can borrow. It tells the story of a young man who embarks on the "Pommern" in Mariehamn and experiences everyday life on board. Yes, life must have been hard almost 100 years ago on such a sailing ship. But the "Pommern" was not a wreck. The shipping company took good care of the crew and their food, as the voice on the audio recording emphasizes. At least those among the crew, presumably the officers, who had been given access to the large bathtub behind the captain's cabin, will not have fared poorly.

At the very bottom of the ship's hold, a unique spectacle awaits visitors: Here the museum has installed a light installation that runs the entire length of the deepest storage. A storm is simulated in shades of blue and with the thunderous roar of waves. Large signs on the stairs warn that this demonstration is not for the faint-hearted. That's right, the hold goes completely dark.

In the maritime museum itself, one can marvel at numerous exhibits. Among all the steering wheels, steam engines, ship models, the captain's saloon of the German sailing ship "Her-zogin Cecilie" that ran into a rock off England in 1936 is particularly striking. A separate section is also dedicated to shipbuilding, showing how wooden ships were traditionally built in the Åland Islands for hundreds of years.

The rain has not let diminished when we step outside the door of the museum. A real storm is passing over us - and what would be the best remedy against such weather in Finland? The sauna, of course. And the sailing club has an exceptionally spacious facility. But you had to find it first: For ladies, the house is south of the clubhouse, for men north of it. The crew of a Finnish yacht has already taken a seat in the sauna. The five young men are all from Helsinki and want to sail through the archipelago for two weeks, as they report, while plenty of water is poured over the stones of the stove for the infusion. And then, as if to fulfil every Finnish cliché, they lift their half-litre beer cans and toast themselves in the sauna. The cans are quickly emptied, and the Finns then jump into the harbour basin to cool off.

During the next sauna session, I meet a Swede who has also come to Mariehamn with his sailing yacht. I estimate him to be in his mid-fifties. But he explains that he has "had enough": enough of working, enough of the "short holidays" that rarely lasted longer than four weeks. I reply that a holiday lasting longer than three weeks in Germany is virtually unthinkable. This surprises the Swedish skipper.

"Svanen" lies in front of the sailing club's restaurant

Nevertheless, he had "enough". With his wife, he bought a sailboat, a respectable "Hallberg Rassy", and they went on tour. Next year they want to take the boat to the Mediterranean and preferably stay there, that's the plan. Well, if one has "had enough" and finds such a way out of his dilemma, I can only congratulate him. The cheerful Finnish crew, who are now also back in the sauna after cooling off, congratulate him on his boat; they have chartered a very similar, pot-bellied "Hallberg Rassy". Next to the elegant club restaurant, this sauna is the social centre of the harbour.

INFO: A VISIT TO THE ONBOARD TOILET

Many new sailors or non-sailors have already asked us whether there is actually a toilet on board. Because this is an important topic, a few comments are due. We have had a bathroom on board every keelboat so far. It is also necessary to not do your business "overboard". The danger of going overboard is too great, especially in heavy seas. That is why we had already equipped our small cruiser with a chemical toilet. It is easy to "install" because it only has to be placed in a free corner, for example, under the companionway. You just put some sanitary liquid in it, and you can use it, including the water flush. The disadvantage: the contents have to be disposed of at some point. The tank is removed from the current models, taken to the port disposal station, and emptied. This is not a tragedy but an unpleasant task. A better solution is, of course, a built-in onboard toilet. The following arrangement is typical: the flushing water is pumped in via a sea valve (i.e. a "closable hole" in the boat), often with a hand pump. The toilet may empty into a separate tank or directly into the water via another seacock. A thick lever on a plastic diverter switch ensures that you empty either straight "out" or into the tank.

In Sweden and Finland, as in some other countries, strict regulations apply: There, faeces may not be disposed of outboard. Therefore, there is a disposal station in almost all plea-sure boat harbours (not in the many fishing harbours). There, a thick hose can be attached to the connection for the tank, which disposes of it. Now the regulations in Germany and Denmark are not so strict for older boats. So if you have a ship without a holding tank, you can use the toilet in this country, but not in Sweden. An alternative is then to carry a small chemical toilet.

Notably, the connections should have a bend, a gooseneck, which will lead the hose higher than the water level beyond the side of the board. Otherwise, it may lead to water entering back into the toilet bowl from the outside. The gooseneck should have a pressure valve at its highest point. If possible, you should close the seacocks to the use, both for the drain and the inlet. However, this is only realistic if the valves are reasonably easy to reach.

Beyond this standard onboard toilet, there are many variations these days: Large and small onboard toilets (most are small), with an electric pump or even vacuum suction. There is something for every budget, although the electric models are always more expensive than those with a hand pump. With the electric pumps, you only have to push a button, which is more convenient. But: If there should be once no more electricity onboard, then the toilet could not be used anymore.

Mr. Moose says: *We moose are not so picky about that business. But I think it's terrific if you don't empty your facilities to the outside anymore. Because when I'm swimming there, I don't want to come across anything that you've brought overboard. Take it back with you and dispose of it on land.*

Mariehamn is a charming town, as it becomes apparent the next day. The rain has temporarily subsided. But it is still storming, which does not always make it easy to pedal on the bikes, which the harbour master has given us free of charge. The city centre stretches between the West Harbour and the East Harbour with its long promenade. With wide streets, relatively low buildings, and lots of greenery, the little town with its 11,000 inhabitants looks more like an affluent suburb than a town in its own right. The streets laid out at right angles date back to a plan from 1859. There are nice shopping streets in the centre and a covered passage where you can escape from the rain showers. Behind there is the "government quarter": there stands the "Lagtings", the parliament of the autonomous province of Åland. Although it is part of Finland, it is Swedish-speaking due to its proximity to Sweden and the archipelago's history, which used to be part of the neighbouring country before becoming part of the Russian Grand Duchy of Finland. Towards the end of the 1880s, Mariehman was to be developed into a spa and bathing resort, and the two avenues of lime trees that criss-cross the town date back to this. The German consulate in the autonomous region of Åland is also located here, somewhat hidden in an inconspicuous house.

But fortunately, we don't have to deal with consular matters. Instead, we rummage through the city with a shopping list for our boat. Among other things, we are looking for a new antenna for the active AIS since the old, self-built antenna no longer provides perfect reception. The boat accessory dealer "Wemarin" has some items in stock we need. The salesman is competent, and he tells me about another German sailor who had passed by here only a few weeks ago and whom he could help with her equipment. I get the antenna, but he doesn't have the cables I need for our navigation in stock either.

The second dealer, a hardware store called "Byggvaruhuset", has a boat department but is neither friendly nor competent. We need tape again to patch the torn weather protection of the furling genoa. The thin plastic tape the salesman holds up looks like it won't last a day on the sail. He explains that he "could have" the other parts, but he doesn't feel like going to the warehouse. I tell him that I don't feel like buying anything then either, to which he shrugs. What the business purpose of this shop at the end of the town actually is, I did not find out any more. It showed again: Once you are on your journey, it is difficult to renew equipment.

Again, the rain whips over the eastern harbour. There we make a coffee stop. Birgit buys beautiful handicrafts in a shop belonging to a small museum harbour on the east side. Mooring here would undoubtedly have been nice, I think, while I look over the rows of moored ships. It's more crowded than at the west harbour. But this one has more character. The gastronomy of Mariehamn can make a few euros turnover with us, as we visit a lovely café in town and a restaurant before we return to our ship in the pouring rain.

On 27 August at 11 am we leave Mariehamn. The wind has calmed down a bit, the weather forecasts are on "green" (maybe also on "yellow"). Between the Åland Islands and the Swedish coast, the forecast is for slightly less swell than further out. The wind comes from the northeast, and our route leads through the lee of the islands. Still in the west harbour, we can set sail and then follow the main path out of the archipelago. In the beginning, the wave forecast of "Predictwind" is correct: The sea is still relatively calm, the wind drives "Svanen" ahead. Unfortunately, the wind direction from astern is what the long keeler does not like so much. And whatever I try - the rolling gets stronger and stronger. Up and down goes the cockpit. I've read a lot about yacht rolling, especially with our long keeler I think it's an important issue. The US-sailor John Kretschmer recommends unfurling the foresail and leaving the mainsail in the second reef in the middle to dampen the rolling. This tactic makes sense. But it doesn't really help us in this situation. The rolling is indeed damped, but only very slightly so that the difference is hardly noticeable.

After a few nautical miles, the protection of the land cover is gone. The waves take on more and more dramatic proportions. I always find it very impressive that when "Svanen" enters a valley between two waves and sitting in the cockpit, you can no longer see the horizon, but only the crest of the next wave rushing in. This and the terribly steep water walls make the ride very exhausting. Sometimes, it seems, the waves break directly above the ship. They dump the seawater into the cockpit. They must be breakers more than two metres high. Fortunately, the waves come from the stern. Sailing into such a sea with the bow would have strained our nerves even more. Hour after hour, we struggle to bring "Svanen" closer to the Swedish coast.

Birgit in the cockpit at sea off Mariehamn

Then the navigation fails again. The "Toughbook" tablet PC, which is clamped to the bulkhead, first loses the connection to the onboard wifi, via which it gets its navigation data. I have always been suspicious of this wifi technology for onboard instruments. But then the screen goes black and stays dark too. What exactly it is, I can't investigate in-depth in this sea state - only that I can't get it to start, and I'm getting fed up with do-it-yourself navigation solutions. But with one swing, I can unfold the old Garmin from the cabin to the front and start the device. And then the tiny five-inch screen shows us precisely the route. True, at the moment, we still have "free sea room", but when we get into the archipelago, I want to have an overview of what's around us at all times. Luckily I built this backup solution on the way there in Nynäshamn.

But now I find the heavy ferry traffic that prevails here somewhat reassuring: Hardly has one of the big ferries passed "Svanen", the next one is already coming. Of course, one has to pay attention to the commercial shipping, but I think that if something should happen to us now, at least a bigger ship would be close by. Fortunately, nothing happens to us. Everything holds on "Svanen". The ship sails like clockwork except for the navigation and the unpleasant rolling. Soon the group of skerries comes into sight, through which we can sail, even if it still takes quite a while until the waves subside and this unpleasant rolling stops. Finally, the ride becomes a bit calmer. It also stops raining. We pass the harbour of "Kappelskär", where we turned north on the way there. Here the circle closes.

Finally, we can again call at the harbour on the island of Lindgren and Strindberg: Furusund. It is much emptier than in the summer, the café is closed, and only a vending machine is available for registration. 41.6 nautical miles was the distance from Mariehamn to here, for which we needed just 7 hours and 30 minutes despite the unpleasant sea. We are back in the Stockholm archipelago.

13 ON THE WAY SOUTH THROUGH STOCKHOLM

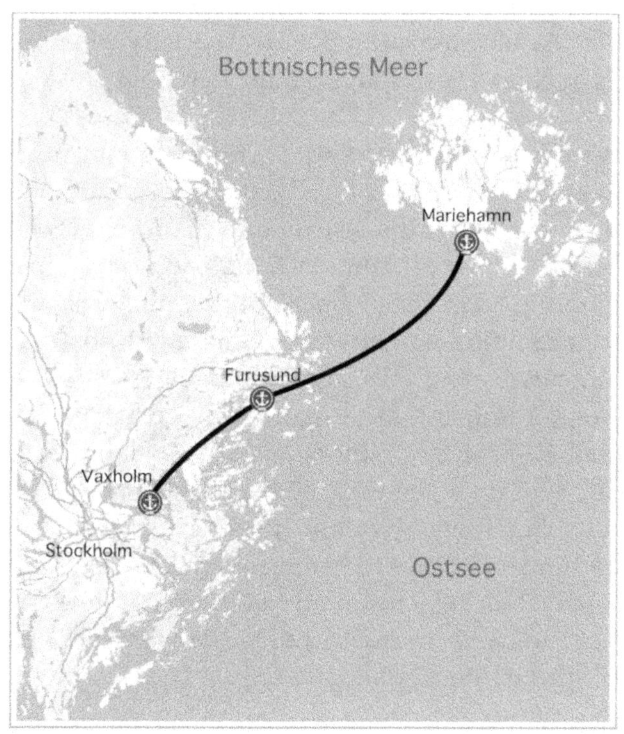

I t is cold and cloudy, but at least it is not raining. We sail back to Stockholm via the northern route through the archipelago. This is the route that we have already chosen on the outward journey. Many ferries travel this fairway. It had been still hot and sunny on the outward journey here, now the weather feels autumnal. While Birgit steers routinely, I sit at the salon table and "roll" online catalogues. My "Hypernetti" card still works in Sweden. This time I programmed the route by hand into the Garmin. The navigation tablet remains unused and dark on the map table. Although the Internet in the EU foreign countries is no longer unlimited, a decent data volume is available. I now want to replace the self-made navigation solution with a chart plotter. After so many nautical miles, I no longer feel like having DIY electronics on board, especially when the weather is as bad as yesterdays on the way from the Åland Islands.

By the way, marine electronics are not even more expensive in Sweden than in Germany, as I find out. Besides Garmin and british B&G devices (on the instruments in our old yacht, the name was still written out: Brooks & Gatehouse), the manufacturer Raymarine offers itself. Since our autopilot is from this company, uncomplicated networking should be possible. And our instruments are from the same company, respectively the predecessor, "Autohelm". They can exchange data via a unique protocol called "Seatalk". Either I get it in Vaxholm at the dealer we already went to on the way there, or I want to go to a special shop. Route planning with public transport is not so complicated in Sweden. And so I picked a connection with a ferry from Vaxholm and a bus, which should fit our arrival time. Because this shop is - not very practical - not located at the water, but at an arterial road of Stockholm.

Archipelago steamers are ubiquitous in Stockholm

The ferries pass again in both directions. Fortunately, there is no checkpoint of the Swedish coast guard today. After just 4 hours and 15 minutes, we pass the fortress in front of the harbour entrance of Vaxholm again. "Svanen" is quickly moored to the mooring lines, which we are now familiar with.

At the ship's chandler, I can inform myself in detail. The young Swede is eager, knows the requirements of a sailor. However, he has no idea where to get the nautical charts needed to operate the plotter. He rummages in his documents, then in the shelves. And suddenly, it turns out that at least the maps of the Swedish coast are included with the plotter.

Back on board, I am impressed: The Raymarine fits immediately on the bracket of the old Garmin, the wiring is done quickly. The device is well thought out and has sailing functions, so I am amazed at what has been done in the ten years since the Garmin was produced. It is pretty impressive what the display shows, such as the wind angle in front of the bow or the "lay lines", which reveal at what angle the next waypoint can best be approached.

I notice: With do-it-yourself electronics, you can achieve quite a lot, for example, steer all the way to Haparanda. But you will always have to deal with failures because these devices are made of components that are not suitable for use at sea. Wind, rain, high humidity and saltwater will always cause problems during use. I would almost prefer pure paper charts. But you can't always read the current position of your own ship on them. And navigating a yacht in unfamiliar waters, i.e. the navigation itself and the sailing, is quite complex, so problems with self-built electronics should not be part of it. But the software continues to run on the laptop, which is well protected in the salon and still makes a good figure for planning.

In Vaxholm, we treat ourselves to a proper dinner at the "Hamnkro", a nice restaurant at the harbour, because tomorrow Birgit has to fly back to Hamburg. Her holiday is over, while I still have the time to bring the boat back to Hamburg. That is a pity, but also on the way there, the "feeder trip" to Stockholm has already worked well. I had planned long before because several routes for the return trip offered themselves: There would have been, of course, the route via Estonia, Lithuania and Poland, and then via Mecklenburg-Vorpommern and the Elbe-Lübeck Canal. But all in all, this route is about 140 nautical miles longer than the route along the Swedish coast. Especially as the eastern course would still involve sailing around Kaliningrad, the Russian exclave on the Baltic Sea. About 100 nautical miles have to be estimated for the route from Lithuania to Poland.

Then there are various combination routes, to Estonia, for example, and further to Latvia, then across the Baltic Sea to Gotland and further to Öland. Or a little along the Swedish coast and then directly south to Gotland. In the end, however, the decision is quite simple: I liked the route from Kalmarsund to Nynäshamn so much on the way here that I would like to sail it again - in the opposite direction from north to south through the archipelago. I am looking forward to this trip. Birgit has chosen the ferry to Stockholm city centre for her trip to Arlanda airport, which leaves regularly from Vaxholm, and then continues with the airport express. After she got on the ferry at 10:15 am, I cast off and head for Stockholm as well, so to speak in the wake of the much faster ferry. But the sun is shining, it is Sunday noon, and a lot is going on on the water. From everywhere boats come, under sail and motor, which provide plenty of variety.

The plan I had laid out was not to work: I wanted to cross Lake Mälaren this time and then switch back to the Baltic at Södertälje. I am looking forward to sailing "Svanen" straight through the town and passing a series of lift bridges. And so I turn from the main fairway into the channel and moor in front of the mighty steel Danviksbron, a railway bridge. Conveniently, an intercom is hanging there, and the bridge keeper tells me that it will open in 30 minutes. I drink a coffee in the cockpit and watch the two other sailors gathered in front of the bridge with a clearance of 11.90 metres. After almost half an hour, there is a flashing light, but the bridge does not open. Instead, there is a crunch on the radio and the attendant talks about "tekniske problems" and that the bridge opening will have to be cancelled. How long it will take, he cannot say yet. With their high masts, the other sailboats set back and leave the channel again. I turn "Svanen" with a heavy heart. Then I will probably have to leave Stockholm the same way we came here.

Disappointed, I steam back along the shore with "Svanen" under diesel, about an hour away is the passage to the south. I pass the huge fountain at Nacka Strand, which has the sonorous name vault of heaven ("Gud Fader på Himmelsbågen"). If I sail "Svanen" now under this water arch, the ship will get a nice shower, I think - but then I don't drift too close to the pier with the base of the sky arch. Small anecdote on the side: We had already tried this once on the Lake Binnenalster in Hamburg with a pedal boat - it was a pretty wet affair.

A little later, I turn to starboard into Skurusundet and chug under an expressway's large bridge construction site. The pretty villas along the steep shore pass by leisurely. When I passed the narrow channel at the deserted bathing place "Boobadet Beach" and set course to Saltsjöbaden, a good mood came up: A nice wind of force 3 blows from southwest, precisely from the right direction. I start to set sail. It's a strange feeling to pull up the sail again now when co-skipper Birgit is not with me.

INFO: AUTOPILOT TAKES THE HELM

Real sailors steer by hand? Not always. You won't want to sit at the wheel or tiller for ten or 14 hours. It's also a question of safety: if you've set a clear course on the open sea, which the autopilot then holds, you can concentrate fully on the surrounding water and other ships instead of constantly squinting at the compass. There are also now more than a few racing sailors who, on ocean crossings, have their vessel steered automatically 99 per cent of the time. If your yacht has a tiller in the cockpit, you will have to resort to Raymarine (formerly Auto-helm) or Simrad models. The Raymarine EVO 100 is one of the few new developments in recent years. An alternative is at most exotics like the "Pelagic" autopilot from the US. If you have wheel steering, there are a few more manufacturers, such as Garmin.

The autopilot is indispensable for longer single-handed trips, as it allows you to keep the boat on course when you need to set sail on the forecastle or make a quick coffee in the galley.

Theoretically, it would also be possible to balance the boat by the sail trim between foresail and mainsail to go straight on its own. With long keelers, this is even more possible than with short keelers. But this is quite an effort and still no guarantee for a clean course. A modern autopilot can also steer by waypoints. This is useful: If we have set a point, say off the coast of Langeland in Denmark, "Svanen" can head precisely to this point. Via the instruments, the course computer not only takes into account course and speed, but also wind direction, wind data and drift. If the current in the Great Belt is 2 knots from south to north and you want to head southwest at an angle, you will see on the display how the autopilot corrects - and you will reach your exact point.

Of course, it would be ideal to have an additional wind steering system on board. You can often admire these on the stern of seagoing yachts, and they already make the ship look like "great sailing". A wind vane at the stern controls an auxiliary rudder in the water, the power of which is, in turn, redirected to the actual rudder blade. Their advantage: they do not need electricity and steer precisely on longer strokes - as long as the wind is blowing. In practice, the opinions of sailing experts differ here. While the German blue-water sailor Bobby Schenk considers a combination of electric autopilot and wind steering system to be ideal, his US colleague John Kretschmer has a different opinion: He simply takes two electric autopilots with him on his trips. And that's how we do it on "Svanen": at least on the coasts, the electric autopilot is enough for us. But we also carry a spare autopilot with us.

Mr. Moose says: I like autopilots. Or at least boats that run under autopilot. Why? Because then you can keep a straight line. Few things make me as nervous in the water as a boat that goes back and forth and

keeps changing course. You feel the same way when you see other boats. When someone stays on course, it's nice and predictable, not just for moose that swim.

When I'm at the front of the mast, I like to use the crank for the winch. You can grab it so nicely and elegantly crank up the mainsail. It's a bit like clockwork, with all the wheels meshing together. And when it's almost up, you can add tension with the crank. Now the sail is up, without reefing, and I climb back into the cockpit to open the furling genoa. And "Svanen" happily picks up speed. Some Swedish weekend sailors overtake me with their bigger boats while I, in turn, leave smaller yachts behind. So everything is in perfect order. I'm not fast, the log, the instrument for the speed through the water, shows 4,5 to 5 knots, but that's enough to reach the harbour of Dalarö comfortably in the afternoon. That's what the Raymarine plotter tells me, on which I marked out the new course earlier, before leaving the berth in front of the defective railway bridge. And now it shows the precise time of arrival. However, the fact that the date is relatively large in the display is a bit annoying. I want to arrive today. We are not sailing across the ocean. I have to try out many commands later in the submenu until the display is correct as I want it.

The second harbour of Dalarö is the "Hotelbrygga", which lies right in front of the fairway. I want to moor there since we already know the other one. It is fun to sail the same route in the opposite direction. However, the harbour is deserted this Sunday evening: A few local motorboats are moored there, but no guests. On the phone the harbour master tells me that he is also surprised that nobody comes. That is unusual. I could move to the other harbour of Dalarö. There is more going on, he tells me. But I find the place between the finger piers that "Svanen" has taken now actually quite good. And there is a nice kiosk at the

"Hotelbryggan". The harbour master is pleased about the call, that doesn't seem to happen often. He explains that he will come by tonight to collect the fee. However, he did not show up anymore.

When the sun has sunk, I plan the route. On the way back I will skip Nynäshamn, the "next stop", and go directly to Oxelö-sund, which I cut on the way there. It is an industrial town south of Stockholm that promises to be interesting. Piece by piece, I put the waypoints on the screen. Well, that's a sporty 54 nautical miles, after all. I switch to "route" mode, which involves longer stages than when we were still strolling around the Bothnian Sea. That means getting up early in Dalarö.

14 THE ÖSTERGÖTLAND ARCHIPELAGO

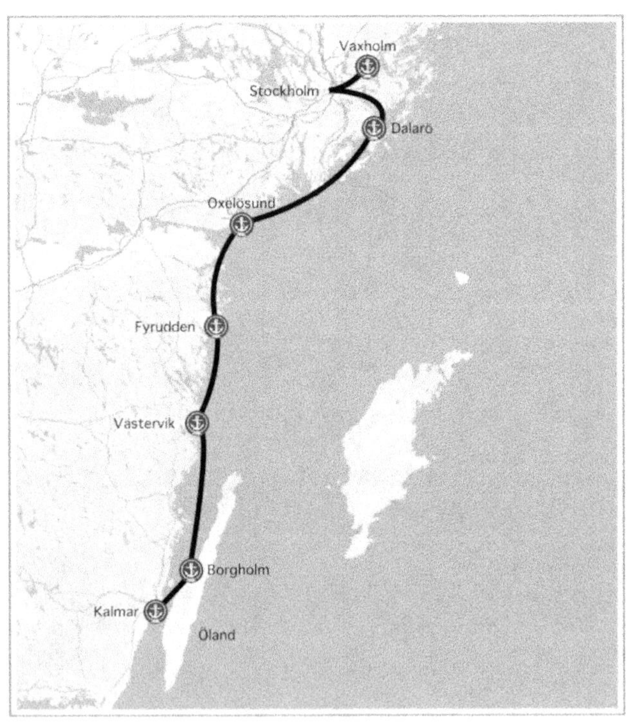

Between Dalarö and Nynäshamn, I hear a bang the next day, which I can not assign. I set off early. It is uncomfortable with 13 degrees Celcius, and there is hardly any wind. So "Svanen" runs under the engine. Another bang. And there I see a Swedish naval ship off the coast, with clouds of smoke coming out of its gun barrels. It is surrounded by two small inflatable boats. Boom, another bang. So it's a military exercise. Impressive: Nothing is announced on the VHF radio, and on the AIS the naval ships cannot be seen because they do not transmit their position. It gets more exciting when the naval ship sets course strictly for "Svanen". The bow is actually heading towards me while the gun continues to bang and emits clouds of smoke. I wonder if there's really ammunition involved. Just to be on the safe side, I take the radio, but then the ship turns away and rushes past on the port side. Maybe they just wanted to show presence to the sailor with the German flag.

The cold of the morning is long gone. When I pass Nynäshamn, the large ferry port south of Stockholm, around noon, it is hot, and the sun is beating down from the sky like it hasn't for many days. The last time we had weather like this was off the Finnish coast. Somewhat wistfully, I steer the route through the archipelago. I had mastered the first leg here in the difficult wind and sea conditions in June, and now I'm on my way back again. But since this time, I don't want to "cut it short" over the sea, but instead take the bow out along the coast, so to speak, the trip promises to be more interesting.

This already starts in the small group of islets, which I had crossed on the way to Nynäshamn on the outward journey. If you stay on the northern shore, you pass a small fishing village, which today probably serves more for tourism. Then a long piece follows straight ahead past a beacon. Finally, the route goes at Kallvik into a dreamlike, small archipelago landscape. I've long since got the sails up again, but the wind didn't really get going today. A little bit with three knots through the archipelago is all that is possible under sail on this day. Then the wind takes off again. But this part of the route is as beautiful as the archipelagos we have already crossed. The islands are tiny and rise up on both sides of the fairway. Again and again, motorboats and more prominent sailors anchor between the rocks.

Nevertheless, the route becomes a bit long in the afternoon, no matter how beautiful the archipelago may be. Therefore, I am more than relieved when finally the harbour facilities of Oxelösund come into sight. The description from the coastal handbook is correct: It is an industrial harbour, but not necessarily unpleasant. Close I take "Svanen" along a quay with cargo ships. There comes the entrance to the guest harbour. I have never experienced this before. There is a huge harbour with four long jetties - and not a single guest boat. But, further back, a small motorboat is moored at the jetty. No doubt: The season is already over up here, still close to Stockholm. I have free choice and choose an excellent place for "Svanen" in the middle of the pier. At the machine, I pay the mooring fee and connect the electricity.

Then my eyes fall on the tin of teak oil I bought in Mariehamn, and I don't grasp the best idea, as would later become apparent. The city is too far away, nothing is going on in the harbour - so why not just oil the teak deck? Especially as the oil is an attractive colour, almost going orange. Besides, "Svanen" is in dire need of a refreshing coat of paint. The last few weeks in the sun have taken their toll on the wood.

In the archipelago off Oxelösund

First, I scrub the cockpit thoroughly. The water hose is ready at the jetty. Then I paint a piece, another piece and before I realise it, I'm already painting the entire cockpit with the oil. In the back of my head, a voice says, though: I hope it dries by tomorrow. But I remember that last time, with a different teak oil from Germany, it took less than 12 hours for the oil to dry. Meanwhile, aggressive mosquitoes are hunting me, so that a good portion of Autan from the bottle in the ship is used.

I think anecdotes also live from mistakes that the author makes. The next morning I recognised the problem right away, and at that moment I don't find it so funny anymore. The entire cockpit is still dripping wet with oil, even though it has had time to dry overnight. Indeed, the colour is great: the teak has taken on a nice reddish hue, better than any other oil I've used before. But it's wet.

While I am still thinking about proceeding, a swanky yacht

approaches the jetty and stops right behind "Svanen". I wonder what they are up to now. Two skippers jump ashore and ask me for the WC code. Well, I am a friendly sailor and give them the code. They will have had an exhausting night trip, I think, so they could do with a shower.

No, it's not like that: they've anchored nearby and now want to use the sanitary facilities. Now I have my doubts. Although they own quite a large yacht, they save on mooring fees, then go into the harbour and ask a comparatively small boat, which has properly paid for the sanitary code. Is that really necessary? That has something of fare evasion, I think somewhat amused, but wish them a good trip anyway.

Then I cover the cockpit with old dishtowels before I start to cast off. But it should still take two days until the deck is completely dry again. And of course, I had orange stains on my old jeans to remind me of the action. But when "Svanen" later went into winter storage, the deck still had that nice orange colour.

If you leave Oxelösund to the south, you drive over the Bråviken. This beautiful expansive sound reaches far inland, up to Norrköping. Then one passes the Slätbaken, also a sound. The Göta-canal flows into it. In this, one could drive elegantly across Sweden to the west coast.

On the way here, I skipped this channel for two reasons: First, I wanted to sail along the archipelago on the Swedish east coast because we already know the western Swedish archipelago well. And secondly, the canal administration charges a handsome fee of over 500 euros for sailing in only one direction. In addition, we had already gained a lot of canal experience in the waters around Berlin. It's not that appealing to chug along an artificial waterway with a sailing boat. Now, at the end of August, it would, of course, be a consideration to use the canal. But then I would be in Gothenburg and would have to sail south along the Kattegat, which I also know. Besides, the boats are divided into columns at this time of year, which pass through one after the other at a brisk pace. So I leave the Slatbäken to starboard and look forward to the archipelago coast, which I want to cross from north to south.

The wind plays along: It comes from a good direction from the west and blows with force four. I have already hoisted the sails shortly after Oxelösund. Now they stand perfectly in a blue sky, from which the sun shines warmly. It is beautiful up here, and the sound is quickly behind me. Then I sail through the archipelago again, and it seems just as beautiful as the first time. I pass the island with the nature reserve Stora Lunda and head for Axelösund. Unforeseen, I have already passed the pretty harbour, between the boulders you could not even see it.

A true sailing dream follows: A constant wind from the west drives "Svanen" on her course to the south. I make myself comfortable at the tiller and steer silently through the archipelago. All I have to do is stick to the route I have programmed into the Raymarine beforehand. And the wind even picks up a little while I'm well protected between the islands.

The destination is the port of Fyrudden, which lies in the middle of the archipelago. On the outward journey, I had already passed it. There were some buildings, a ferry dock for the archipelago steamers, which are still sparse here, and many countries' pier flags are flying. It looked very inviting, including the harbour restaurant. The route is a comfortable 32 nautical miles, each of which I enjoyed. Shortly before Fyrudden, I recover the sails. There is more wind outside the harbour, so I am pretty glad when I have stowed them safely.

I am almost speechless: Not a single guest boat has moored in this pretty harbour. At the hut of the harbour master hangs a sign that the harbour will be closed on September 1st at the end of the season, exactly at 6 pm. It is not 6 pm yet, but half an hour before, but it is already closed. Also the small supermarket, the lovely restaurant and the café. That's it for the 2021 season in Fyrudden. Even if the showers are closed at least one toilet is still open. And the water? It is with 15 degrees Celcius no longer suitable for a comfortable bath.

Nevertheless, there is some life in the harbour: Two water taxis are still running, which bring the residents to their holiday homes in the archipelago. They rattle out of the port and a little later back in again, making a lot of swells. When it gets dark, they stop operating. I plan the next stage. How about somewhere a little busier for a change? Västervik is a nice little town. Surely something will still be open there. A supermarket would not be bad for provisions. The route is quickly planned and mapped out.

It's 34 nautical miles from Fyrudden to Västervik, and I call the next day "the great tour of the blue coast". Because there is simply everything: The route winds between the archipelago and leads twice to the open sea, where there is not enough depth between the islands. The weather forecast from the evening before keeps its promise: It is sunny, and the wind blows steadily. Only on the sections on the open sea, it increases a little. And because the wind has turned to the east, big waves come rolling in. But the boat can ride off these waves without any problems. I remember many a narrow passage from the outward journey, impressive houses standing between woods and rocks on the shore. Somehow I feel at home in this section. If you want to get to Stockholm or Finland from central Europe, you can bask in the thought that part of the journey will take you through the most beautiful archipelago imaginable. Indeed, it may be an option to call at Gotland. But I wouldn't trade any other route for this one.

Västervik is hidden between the archipelago. Nothing about the passage between two large islands hints that a small town is coming soon. Only when one turns around the next archipelago, there are more houses at the shore, and soon harbour facilities come into view. There is a sign missing, one could think, even if everything is written on the sea chart. The guest harbour promises to be a bit expensive. On the net, it advertises with its modern pontoons, with delivery service for food and the expensive hotel. After three nights in deserted harbours, I'd be in the mood for a bit of a spectacle. But you can't expect much life here at the beginning of September. There are at least a few guest boats at the piers, a friendly German sailor helps to moor "Svanen".

Behind it are a hotel and an apartment complex. The investor is the now 76-year-old Björn Ulväus from Abba, who comes from Västervik and has donated modern architecture to his town here. By the way, Västervik calls itself a "summer city". I don't know a similar expression in German, but it works: The whole place is geared towards summer and guests.

The modern guest harbour of Västervik

There is, for example, the pretty harbour promenade that lies behind a bascule bridge or the alleys in the old town where restaurants and cafés have set up their tables and chairs. It is more than just a holiday resort, a "summer town" in fact. Only that according to Swedish reckoning, September is no longer summer, the many cafés are empty in any case. Unfortunately, the supermarket is located at the other end of the city centre. It is a nice walk. But on the way back with well-filled shopping bags, it's a bit of a scramble. But never mind, I feel very comfortable in Västervik with its "off-season" atmosphere.

The next morning's petrol station, two nautical miles south of the guest harbour, is also quickly reached. The diesel supplies replenished, I can continue south. In this case, of course, sailing because the wind from the east fits again. There is a long distance to cover today. I want to see how far I can get into the Kalmarsund.

The course through the archipelago fairway is not always ideal for the wind, but sometimes the islands take the swell almost entirely away. Nevertheless, I make good speed with the Vindö 32. And what is that? Shortly before the end of the archipelago fairway, "Svanen" overtakes a Vindö 40, very slowly but noticeably, which has hoisted the same sails. Then I move up to a Swedish Folkboat from behind. With the Swede who sits there at the helm, I can exchange a few words until I slowly pass.

Suddenly, the archipelago is over, I come out between the two islands, which I still remember well from the outward journey. Here begins the Kalmar Sound. The dreamy trip between the islands is over. A strong wind of force five blows and decent waves come from the northeast into the sound. I brace myself, but decide not to reef yet. The autopilot takes over and heads for the next waypoint that the Raymarine plotter tells it to. It's going to be a roaring ride. "Svanen" ploughs through the waves and "races" south at over six knots. I pass the island "Blå Jungfrun", which rises out of the water like a semicircle in the middle of the Kalmar Sound. Some other sailors pass by in the opposite direction, greeting and waving to each other in a friendly manner. A perfect day to make the distance. Hour after hour passes quickly when you sail as beautifully as I am doing this day. You can feel the ship making its way south, and even as the sun sinks lower and I sail past Öland, I don't feel like stopping. But another problem arises as the sun slowly approaches the horizon: The lighting seems to have a malfunction. At the mast, the white "steamer lantern" is shining, and also, at the stern, the white bulb lightens up. But the two lamps at the bow, which still worked during the last test a few days ago, remain dark. "Svanen" has an old and a new switchboard. The new one supplies power to the navigation instruments, while the old panel is responsible for the lighting. While the autopilot holds course, I look through the fuses and clean the contacts. Nothing, no light ahead. I consider heading for the port of Sandvik, to which I am now abeam.

Fortunately, the waves have subsided behind Öland. I carefully go to the bow and examine the lamps. Nothing to discover. But because it will soon be seriously dark, light is needed. The distributor is in the anchor locker, and I decide on a pragmatic solution: run a cable from this distributor to the mast base above deck. There is the plug for the deck lighting, which I can do without. After quickly connecting the cable, I try the switch - and everything lights up. A nice feeling: The instruments shine, the compass glows red, behind the white light and in front, green and red, as it should be. Equipped like this, I can cover the last nautical miles to the harbour of Borgholm. 56.5 nautical miles exactly, for which I needed 10.5 hours.

Borgholm is said to be a "party hotspot" in the summer, with so many boats calling that they have to be tightly packed. Then the party goes on all night. But today - you guessed it - the harbour is as good as empty as I enter in the darkness, guided by solid fires ashore. Here a friendly Swedish motorboat driver is standing by at the jetty, helping to take on the lines.

"You must be a tough guy," he says, "to come out here alone in your sailboat in this weather."

"Yes, it was long, but with the wind not so strenuous. Under full sail, I went into the Kalmar Sound."

"That's the advantage with a sailboat. With us, it was swaying quite a bit," he counters, pointing to his motorboat. It's pretty with its long, elegant lines, and he's just bought it.

"I use it to go back and forth between Kalmar, where I live, and my weekend home near Västervik." An excellent idea:

visiting your own weekend home in the archipelago by boat. Whereby he could only step on the gas in the archipelago. But that's where a sailing boat like "Svanen" is in its element: When the wind blows hard, the sails stabilise the boat and it ploughs through the waves rather than being buffeted.

A big attraction of the harbour, at least from my point of view, is the "Strand Hotell". Because there are not only sanitary facilities but also a sauna and swimming pool for harbour guests. But this is too much for one day. When I stand in front of the hotel reception, the swimming pool is long closed. I have completely overlooked that it is already far after midnight. I was fortunate that the Swede on the motorboat has still instructed me.

The leg from Borgholm to Kalmar the next day actually should be a small jump, "lousy" 16 nautical miles, which I want to ride in three hours. But that becomes more exhausting than thought. I can still sail a few miles initially, but in the narrowing sound, the wind turns and now comes almost from the front towards me. In addition, steep waves have built up precisely from the front. It rocks and swings. This is not a stable ride like yesterday. "Svanen" climbs laboriously along the Kalmarsund to the south, until after four hours and 15 minutes, the sign at the harbour entrance, directly behind the bridge from the mainland to Öland, comes into view: Kalmar is written there in big letters. Gratefully I chug into the harbour.

I am surprised that there are guests in the harbour again. There are quite a few places free, but many German sailors are arriving gradually. This must be because we are now much further south and again come into the radius of Baltic sailors from Germany, for whom September is still the season.

And in the process, it comes to unpleasant scenes: A sailor couple on a brand new GRP-yacht, wearing expensive clothing and with the best equipment, manages to moor after endless attempts just barely. I am actually not a friend of the "harbour cinema", on the contrary, one would like to be somewhat strangely ashamed. But it's the newest and fanciest ships that tend to go wrong.

As if to confirm this, a large yacht crashes into the quay wall the next moment. The skipper grumbles loudly. He finds it impossible that there is no staff in this harbour to help him moor. Where might he have built up this expectation?

In Kalmar, besides many attractions, there is also an essential address for sailors: "Baltik Skeppsfournering" is the name of the ship chandler right at the harbour, which enjoys an excellent reputation. I am looking for a connecting sea chart outside Sweden for the Raymarine plotter. And the man who looks after the charts at Baltik is literally pulling out all the stops. He phoned suppliers to see if he could find a suitable chart of Denmark and Germany, whether it came from C-Map or Navionics. When he has found the map, he drives off to pick up the chip. A little later, while I am waiting at the harbour, my phone rings and the map is there. The price also fits so much service: the electronic nautical chart with the broad coverage is cheaper at "Baltik" than at the mail-order companies in Germany, as a glance at the Internet shows me. So they still exist, the good ship chandlers.

The stay in Kalmar is as pleasant as last time, with the difference that the motorboats do not do "soundchecks" today and no parties. The supermarket in the shopping centre "Baronen" at the harbour has the necessary provisions. And in the city, there are so many open restaurants that it is hard to choose. Kalmar is simply a good stopover on the way north. It's a beautiful city with lots to see, like Kalmar Slot or Stortorget, but it's also an excellent place to get provisions. Kalmar has a lovely harbour, and it is fun to stroll through the old town streets with their many shops. And the Kalmarsund is a comfortable, sheltered waterway on the way along the Swedish east coast.

In full sail as darkness falls on the Kalmarsund

15 FROM THE SOUTH COAST OF SWEDEN TO DENMARK

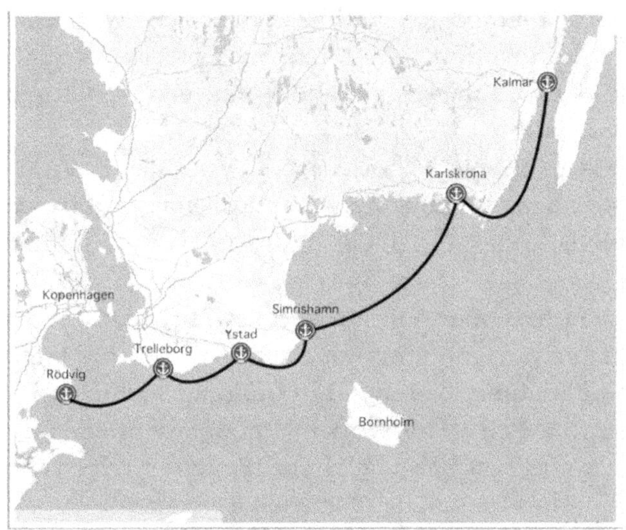

I f you sail between the Kalmar Sound and the Swedish south coast, you can, of course, take the route via Utklippan. I stopped on the lonely island in the Baltic Sea on the way here. Or one chooses the path over Karlskrona, leading deep into the Hanö Bugt. This is the route I am aiming for now. I have a little chat with my German neighbours. "All the way to Karlskrona today, that far?" the neighbour asks me. I explain that I'll see how far I can get. After all, there are some very nice harbours in the Kalmarsund. But the destination is Karlskrona.

The wind blows unsteadily. With help from the engine, I run the first leg of the route through the sound to the south. Then I set sails. I pull up everything I can, and yet "Svanen" just creeps down the sound. An hour is sailed at three knots. If there were endless time, I would leave it at that. But the plotter signals me incorruptibly that the arrival time at this speed will be long after midnight. Again, I don't want that. Such precise calculations have also changed the sailing a bit. So the engine has to be used for the trip south.

There is an excellent shortcut to Karlskrona via a route that is not immediately obvious on the nautical chart, but the coastal handbook describes it in detail. There are three routes into the city, one from the east, one from the west and the main fairway from the south. If one comes from the north out of the Kalmarsund, one can navigate through a very well buoyed fairway to the island Långören, then wind through the archipelago of Karlskrona up to the city. This works without any problems. The bridge that you pass has a height of 18 metres, which should not cause any issues for smaller yachts like "Svanen".

What then, I think, again an archipelago here in the south? Yes, but the islands are small with green shores, some with beaches, like you might find in Denmark. There are deciduous trees on them, unlike in the north. Nevertheless, they are made of granite. In this respect, there is definitely an archipelago near Karlskrona, but it looks pretty different from the north.

The approach to the naval city is beautiful, because you can see the Fredrikskyrkan from far away. This large church with its two towers stands out from the many houses in the city. The route through the archipelago has saved about five nautical miles compared to the route from the south, i.e. 54 instead of 59 nautical miles. So I arrive in Karlskrona halfway in time with the evening light.

The guest harbour Talebryggan is located in a redeveloped harbour area. The crew, sailing on a German sailing school from Berlin, helps with mooring. The port offers every comfort and is - what a wonder - again poorly visited. Because the laundry is included in the price, I take the opportunity to wash in the evening and then use the efficient dryers. The drums hum evenly in the bright and clean sanitary building while I inspect the sauna. I hesitate but then decide not to take a sauna in the evening. So a little later, I have a big pile of fresh laundry on board. The noise from the expressway, which the coastal handbook warns about, is not heard in the outer guest places.

In general, Karlskrona seems to be one single harbour. Clockwise around the island, it looks like this: To the west lies the huge maritime museum, the Naval Museum of Sweden. Its pride is the "Jarramas", a three-master that served as a sail training ship of the Swedish Navy from 1901 to 1939. Behind the museum, there is also a tiny guest harbour. In the south, there is the bastion Aurora and behind it, the only extensive Swedish naval base on the island of Lindholm, which cannot be reached as a civilian neither from land nor sea. In the east, there are the islands of Saltö and Eckholmen. Behind them, there is a vast harbour for leisure boats at the islet of Stakholmen. The Talebryggan, with its guest harbour, is located in the north of the island with the city that is connected with the mainland by the mentioned highway and a railway embankment.

In 1679 Karlskrona was founded as a rather cleverly designed base for the Swedish fleet. King Charles XI, with Admiral Hans Wachtmeister, implemented the plan, which was to surround the city with water on all sides, making it easily defensible. More than 30 islands were built for this purpose. In 1790, however, a large part of Karlskrona burned down. The rebuilt city is also called a baroque city. For its 33.000 inhabitants, Karlskrona looks quite urban, even if not all buildings are historical baroque buildings. Again and again, somewhat rough brick houses from the fifties and sixties rise between the older buildings. With an e-scooter, here the brand "Bird" is offered, all sights can be easily navigated: You roll-off, then simply park, log out on the smartphone and continue the journey later. For example, there is an impressive square in front of the Fredrikskyrkan. Next to the baroque church are the library and the courthouse. To the north is Norra Kungsgatan with the city centre, which is quite pretty to explore, but not very large. Behind the naval base, one can visit an interesting small quarter with accommodations of the soldier families over the ramp of the Wachtmeistergatan. There are lovely places to eat in the area around the fish market, where the small fleet of archipelago steamers from Karlskrona departs.

At dinner some cars of the German Bundeswehr park in front of the restaurant and a group of soldiers is sitting at the neighbouring table. They do, what soldiers all over the world do sometimes: They get drunk. One of them explains that he actually finds Sweden quite nice, but one should certainly not expect "German standards" here. What exactly they mean by that is beyond me. Maybe it's the price of the alcohol that bothers him.

Fredrikskyrkan in the centre of Karlskrona

It's time for a hotel stay again and I check into the Scandic Hotel directly at the fish market. The house is an excellent example of modern Scandinavian architecture, not only from the outside but also from the inside: the rooms are very bright but minimalistically furnished. Fun fact: there's no phone anymore, but a card explaining how to reach the reception with your smartphone. And the hotel advertises on a sign that it is "cash-free", here you can only pay with a card.

After two days in Karlskrona, another jump towards the south is on the agenda. Either you sail along the coast towards the island of Hanö, this is the route taken by the German sailing-school from Berlin, or you make a more enormous strike directly to Simrishamn. I decide on the latter way. I rather want to make one considerable lag and then take a break for another day.

Slowly I chug past the maritime museum in bright sunshine and admire the old boats.

Ahead of me lies the exit from Karlskrona and exactly 57.1 nautical miles across the Hanöbugt. The ferry, which is on the way to the offshore island Aspö, honks like crazy behind me. I quickly give way because the fairway is narrow here. But the ferry captain waves friendly from his bridge. I sail into the open Baltic Sea between two Swedish navy ships, which also leave Karlskrona. The way leads between two fortifications from the 17th century, the Drottningskärs Kastell on the western and the Kungsholms Fort on the eastern skerry. You can already guess how well defended this harbour was with its approaches secured by forts.

The wind does not suit my venture, as it blows too weakly again. Although I'm happy about a smooth ride with a slight swell, but where should the speed come from, if not from the diesel? On top of that, there is a current of 1.2 knots upwind, as the instruments tell me. If I don't want to arrive after midnight, according to the forecast from the Raymarine, I have to open the throttle. "Svanen" hums across the Baltic, the sun sinks lower. The island of Hanö is clearly visible, tempting me with a detour, but I continue to head south. Before the sun sinks completely, I see a shadow on the horizon. No doubt, that must be Bornholm. I have already gone that far south. Now for the lighting: I still haven't found a fault, so I have to use the improvised cable from the anchor locker again. But the Vindö shines beautifully in red, green and white. Many fishing boats are drifting in front of Simrishamn. The lighting is all the more critical.

Entering this harbour in the dark is less complicated than expected. Only the mooring at the finger jetty is a little tricky. I courageously climb along the swaying jib and deploy the mooring lines. On the neighbouring yacht, two sailors are sitting in the cockpit reading books in the light of their headlamps. I think such a light wouldn't be impractical, but only to deploy the lines - certainly not to read a book in the cockpit. Their expensive functional clothing with the lamps in the headband look very seaworthy but also a bit silly in the harbour.

"Svanen" lies so beautifully on the jetty that I treat myself to a break the next day. So I have not cast off but remain comfortably on the jetty. I walk through the town, which I know from the way there. The alleys are pleasant to walk. In between, there are small parks and cafes. On "Svanen" in the afternoon, I make "clear ship" again. Then I go to the lovely cafe "Byvägen Simrishamn" at the harbour. Until a few years ago, there was a ferry from here to Bornholm, which has been discontinued in the meantime. In the middle of September, the harbour is deserted. Only the big kiosk is open. Some short stages follow: From Simrishamn to Ystad, from there to Trelleborg and then the jump across the southern exit of the Öresund back to Denmark. The trip from Simrishamn to Ystad is terrific again. The wind blows fresh from the east and drives "Svanen" along the pretty south coast of Sweden. On the way, I first pass the sandy beach with pine forests, in which a lighthouse hides, and then the Swedish military training area with its barren dune landscape.

In Ystad, there is still life: A few yachts have moored in the harbour, most of them from Germany. The town itself is also bustling with activity. Trelleborg, on the other hand, appears a little eerie later on. The actual harbour of the city is exclusively reserved for ferries and cargo ships. Yachts have to go to the leisure harbour of Gislovsläge. On the way, one passes Smygehuk, the southernmost point of Sweden.

Not many boats moored in Simrishamn harbour

There is a guest harbour there, but there is a strange, foul stench over it. So I don't envy the boats that have chosen to moor there. The smell must come from nasty algae that pile up in the outer harbour - I can't find any other explanation.

In Gislovs Läge, on the other hand, nothing is going on. Not a single guest boat has moored at the jetty, just like in the north, although it is only mid-September. The fishermen's huts at the harbour's edge now house small holiday apartments. In a few of them, there is still light. At least the friendly café is open, offering baguettes au gratin, "La Flute" these are called in Germany. At least they also made their way to southern Sweden. At night it gets cold again, and fog rolls in. This dips the dark harbour basin into a milky something, in which the orange glow of the lamps on the shore shines eerily.

Now the departure to Denmark follows. I fetch the small

Danish courtesy from the cupboard (in German sailor latin, it is also called "Schapp" - for whatever reason). I hold it ready. But there is still fog in front of Gislosvs Läge, making it difficult to spot the ferries travelling to Trelleborg. With careful sailing, I pass the harbour at a respectful distance. Here the AIS is a great orientation aid.

Around noon, the fog clears, and the journey across the southern end of the Öresund can begin. First, there is a little cruising in front of the small port of Skårehamn, the last meters of the Swedish coast in sight. But then, things get serious, as there is a lot of ship traffic in the Öresund. Most of the traffic that goes around Skagen along the Danish coast into the Baltic Sea takes the route over the Öresund. Only very deep ships have to divert to the Great Belt further east. The path leads from the north through a traffic separation area, ending in a roundabout. Here there are two "exits" for commercial shipping, to the south and to the east. As a recreational skipper, you have to cross the traffic separation area at right angles, as is taught in the textbook.

It's not that easy: ships are rushing by non-stop, loaded with containers or bulk cargo, with cranes or without, some ferries are there and large tankers. There always seem to be gaps between them, but you have to remember that the freighters are about 20 knots fast, while "Svanen" passes at five to six knots. And you have to estimate whether the next freighter will turn south or east after the "roundabout". But we manage to pass without any problems when there is a slightly more significant gap. I found it even more difficult off Gothenburg, where the commercial shipping also rushes through a "Baltic" route. So now the journey to Denmark can be continued more calmly. A short stopover in the harbour of Rödvig is on the way south. Many Baltic sailors will know this pretty place. It is an ideal stopover, for example, when coming from southern Sweden and when heading north towards Öresund and Malmö or Copenhagen. However, the harbour is always quite crowded, even now in September. In Denmark, the sailing season again seems similar to Germany, quite different from high in the north.

INFO: EVERYTHING REVOLVES AROUND THE SEA WEATHER

Ideal sailing weather turns up rarely. After all, you don't want to be drifting in a lull with slack sails, but you also don't want to encounter wave crests on the North Sea at wind force eight. Now there are many ways to get good weather forecasts. There is the information from the internet, sure. But there are also marine weather reports via radio, as the UK Met office or German broadcast by the marine radio stations of "dp07". In Denmark, however, you will miss these reports due to lack of reception.

Sea weather via radio is no longer of great importance, as the mediumwave transmitters mostly have ceased operation in Europe (not for the BBC, though). There are weather reports via the transmitter Pinneberg of the German Weather Service (DWD) if you have a shortwave receiver: In test mode, it transmits on 5905 kHz and 6180 kHz, at 6 a.m. UTC (coordinated universal time, two hours ahead of Central European Summer Time), at 12 a.m. and 8 p.m. Curious: A computer voice reads out the current weather forecast for the North Sea and the Baltic Sea. The forecasts via the "Navtex" system can also be received by radio, but these are really only very brief messages, usually only for the next day.

But no matter which transmission method you choose to receive your weather forecast, I would encourage you to use a high-quality forecast, and only with healthy scepticism. The problem: There are countless ad-supported apps for smartphones that use free data from the US GFS model for the entire world. But their forecast points are further apart than the European models. Once we were about to cross the Skagerrak, a well-known wind app offered for free predicted friendly force three winds and sun. The Swedish weather service and the DWD warned of force six gusts and poor visibility. And that's exactly what happened when we were at sea in our boat, and the wind whistled around our noses off the western Swedish archipelago - until we turned back again.

My lesson: First of all, I trust the national weather services, whether it's the UK Met Office in the UK, the German weather service DWD or the Swedish SHMI. That's where I know meteorologists have done their research on the weather while the free apps "bang out" a purely machine-generated forecast. Even elaborate, colourful graphical displays on smartphones don't cut it. I'd rather have a simple forecast, say in the style of the DWD, with sea area, forecast time, wind direction and wind strength than a bright animation based on the GFS.

The problems with the inaccuracy of the free US model on our coasts are also confirmed by the experts from the European Centre for Medium-Range Weather Forecasts (ECMWF). Their own model has a higher resolution on our shores. The British also have their own model with the "UKMO", and there are also unique models like "Arome" or "Spire" from France. Forecasts with such models can also be obtained very easily via apps on your smartphone. Or you can download the data as so-called "Grib" files via the internet, which you can view on your onboard laptop or chart plotter.

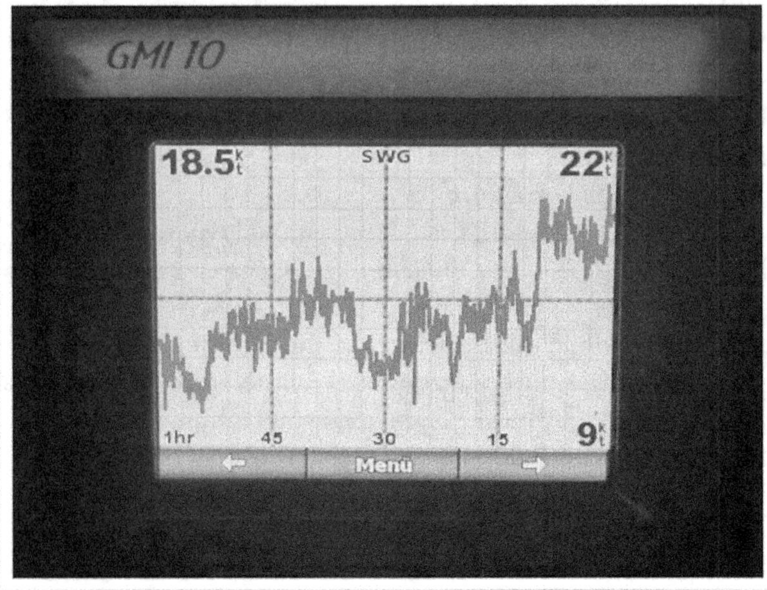

Gloomy outlook: Here the instrument shows how
the wind has increased in one hour

If you use ECMWF as forecast, you are already much better
positioned than with the GFS. An app that combines many
models is "Predictwind". Other recommended providers are
"Windy" and "Meteoblue". Even with a free account, you can get
by relatively well with these on European coasts. You should
always look at another one no matter which forecasts you prefer.
For example, you could compare the Danish forecast of the DMI
with the German one of the DWD. Or you could look at the
ECMWF model and compare it with the UKMO.

Mr. Moose says: *We moose sense the weather coming our way. We don't like snowstorms, for example. We descend into the valleys when it gets too cold in winter to find food among the snow-covered trees. And when it's too hot in summer - we don't handle heat very well - we move up into the mountains - or take a refreshing dip in a lake, a river or the sea. So if I had something like weather forecasts for moose, I'd use those too. And remember: don't rely on just one source. Always consult several. And here is one more hint from an experienced moose: You better add another wind force on top of it at the end. So, if you don't want to experience more than wind force six on the next leg of your trip, make sure that the forecast in your sea area doesn't exceed five Beaufort. That way, you still have a reserve of lousy weather.*

16 A VISIT TO COPENHAGEN

Here, at the southern exit of the Öresund, Copenhagen is not far away. It is 24 nautical miles by boat from the "roundabout" with its traffic separation areas directly to Copenhagen city centre. We visited the city twice. I sailed past it in the south on the trip to Haparanda, but if you have time, you should not miss Copenhagen. The city has a different character than, say, Stockholm. It is even more open, cheerful and colourful than the Scandinavian cities further north.

For sailors, there are no less than four mooring options in the Danish capital: In the north of the city lies Tuborghafen, a very modern facility for recreational skippers. It was built on an area similar in architecture to the Hafencity in Hamburg. This was formerly the site of the Tuborg brewery. I mention the marina for the sake of completeness and because the Royal Danish Yacht Club is located there. I don't find the harbour particularly attractive, despite the modern architecture. The railway station in Hellerup is 1.5 kilometres from the harbour - that would be the connection to Copenhagen city centre.

We liked the "Svanemøllehavnen" (Internet: smhavn.dk), which we also visited, much better. This complex is located south of Tuborghavn, between the "Strandvejskvarteret" district and the island of "Nordhavn", where there is a lot of construction activity. Here, too, new offices, shops and flats are being built in the style of Hafencity. The harbour itself is huge, with over 1,200 berths operated by several sailing clubs and extending to a pier head with a walkway. Moorings are on berths with a "green" sign. The connection to the S-Bahn (Svanemøllen station) is better than in Tuborg harbour. The "Café Sundet" in the north of the marina is particularly nice. There is a large terrace and a light-flooded interior on the first floor of the clubhouse, where you can also get good food. By the way, the harbour advertises that the other two restaurants of the sailing clubs also offer good and inexpensive food. Here you can visit the big city and lie in the midst of active sailors.

Nearby, the blue and white ferries of DFDS moor at a new terminal connecting Copenhagen with Oslo. They look quite attractive, not too big and massive, like the huge ships that sail to Norway from Germany. But we are sailing on our own keel, and ferries like cruise ships are not our profession - we let the big ships go.

But what if you now sail further into the city, by boat? That's what we did. First comes the harbour on Langelinie with the walkway that leads out of the city centre along the water and where the Little Mermaid stands. It is clearly more tourist-oriented than the two northern harbours: here there are only guest moorings, in the north you moor on free spaces next to the permanent moorings.

However, the biggest attraction in the search for a nice mooring is in the district of Christiania. There, canals run through the district, directly along the streets. The whole thing is reminiscent of the canals in Amsterdam - but unlike there, visitors can moor here with sailing yachts or motorboats. We drove through it with and had a look. It's a wonderfully relaxed atmosphere: the residential houses stand along the road, in front of them are the quays where the boats are moored - close together, many hundreds of metres one after the other. Sometimes, though, when a low bridge comes along that doesn't open at the moment, it's the end of the line for yachts with masts. Now the quarter is very hip and the places are in demand. Even if you come around noon, there's hardly a chance of a place in the high season, so it's correspondingly difficult to lie in Copenhagen's centre.

The best place would be the famous "Nyhavn" in the middle of the city with its many restaurants, pubs and cafés on the quays opposite. But getting a berth here would be like winning the lottery: most of the ships moored there don't move away very quickly, and most of them are larger, traditional sailing ships. I only mention Nyhavn as a berth for the sake of completeness. From there it is only a stone's throw to the city centre with its attractions. But you can also walk into the city from Langelinie or, for example, take the train from the northern harbours.

„LANDGANG" IN COPENHAGEN

The city of Copenhagen is located on the water. But it is not as clearly located there as it is in Hamburg, Gothenburg or Oslo. The many islands and canals can make orientation difficult, a bit like in Stockholm. But you can find your way around: The two "fixed points" of the city centre are Nyhavn in the east and Tivoli with the main railway station in the west. In between, you stroll through the numerous streets of the city centre.

We walk along the Langelinie from the "Kastelet", the fortress right by the harbour, into the city. On the way, we pass Amalienborg Palace. The beautiful palace is located right next to Amalienhafen harbour. Four identical buildings make up the palace complex: There is the palace of Christian the VII, that of Christian the VIII, of Frederik the VIII and finally that of Christian the IX. So each of these kings got his own palace. Amalienborg Palace is where the Danish Queen lives. And just as in Buckingham Palace, you know that Her Majesty is at home when the flag is raised. Incidentally, the Palais Christian VIII can be visited, because the "Amalienborg Museum" is located there.

From 11.30 a.m., visitors can also witness the changing of the guard of the Life Guards. The soldiers march from their barracks at Rosenborg Palace through the city to Amalienborg, where they change the guard with some pomp at 12 noon. When Her Majesty the Queen is staying at the Palais Christian IX, the changing of the guard is celebrated with particular pomp, and the Danish flag is also carried. There are several other ceremonies, depending on whether other members of the royal family are present at Amalienborg or none of them are there. Admittedly, this is then the smallest replacement.

Directly behind the castle stands the striking Frederik's Church, also known as the Marble Church. With its large dome, it shapes the silhouette of the city, but its history is also a little tragic: the foundation stone was laid in 1749 by King Frederik the V, but in 1770 his successor King Christian the VII stopped the construction. For a long time, the church was a ruined building standing in the middle of Copenhagen. Only after a hundred years did things continue: in 1874, the Danish state sold the shell to the industrialist Carl Frederik Tietgen. He completed the church according to the old plans, handed it over to the state - and received the neighbouring land in return. A visit to the church with its magnificent interior with lots of marble and the two organs is of course still worthwhile today.

Right next door is the Museum of Decorative Arts (designmuseum.dk), which displays industrial design, works of art and design from Denmark - a good destination for any design lover. The friendly museum has an old and a new building, both of which are great places to spend a few hours: From fashion to household items to furniture, you can see many examples of successful design. A museum shop and a nice café are of course also part of the museum. In Grønnegaard Park, right behind the building, you can sit on benches and enjoy a coffee from the museum.

Before we turn our attention to the city centre, we don't want to miss a brief visit to the second castle in Copenhagen. Another castle? Yes, "Rosenborg" was built in 1606 to 1607 by Christian IV as a so-called pleasure palace. However, the royal family only lived there until 1720. The castle became a historical museum as early as 1838. It lies just "behind" Amalienborg and the marble church in the northwest and is surrounded by a beautiful park in the style of the Dutch Renaissance, right in the middle of the big city. Inside the palace, visitors are fascinated by the Knights' Hall, which includes a real throne. The famous tapestries depicting King Christian V's victory in the war for Scania against Sweden also hang there. On the ground floor are three treasure chambers containing the crown jewels and Denmark's royal insignia.

But now on to modern Copenhagen: two stops away by bus, or a good one and a half kilometres on foot, we come across the main railway station. If you arrive in Copenhagen by train (or S-Bahn), you're bound to stumble into Tivoli. Such amusement parks have been popular in Scandinavia for a long time, as we were to see in Gothenburg and also Stockholm. According to the tourist information office, Tivoli is "Denmark's most popular attraction", attracting over four million visitors a year. It advertises "wild rides, great restaurants, concerts and theatre performances". The park was opened as early as 1843 and Walt Disney is said to have had Tivoli in mind when he designed "Disneyland" in the 1950s. Queen Margrethe II celebrated her 50th anniversary on the throne in May 2022 at Tivoli: the 82-year-old enthusiastically rode the roller coaster.

Children are thrilled not only by the carousels but also by the imaginative figures of the "Tivoligarde" with musical instruments. And when it gets dark, the park becomes very romantic, thanks to the many illuminations in the park. Such details ensure that Tivoli is altogether more sophisticated than some other amusement parks.

Afterwards, we dive into "Strøget", the pedestrian zone that runs right through the city centre. To be honest: Coming straight from the direction of the station, it doesn't seem particularly original at first. There are the usual chains with clothes like in many big cities, in between slightly scruffy tourist shops with souvenirs and exchange offices. The much-cited "hygge feeling" that the tourist information promises is not yet to be found here. Fortunately, this impression dims the further west you walk and especially when you turn into the side streets. In Nørregade, for example, things get more interesting: It branches off towards the university and is followed by some original cafés where it is worth taking a break.

Back on the way to Strøget, a visit to "A.C. Perch's Thehandel" is a good idea, as this shop on Kronprinsengade is right on our way. Now this is really "hygge": The shop is one of the oldest shops in Copenhagen. Since it opened in 1835, the interior has remained original, with shelves of green wood in English colonial style. We buy a pack of "Earl Grey" for Birgit and a bag of ginger tea for me, which we will drink later on our boat.

Not far from Strøget, we want to take a look at some design again and pay a short visit to the shops of Georg Jensen, Royal Copenhagen and the no less noble "Illums Bolighus". There you can find household goods, but also lamps and furniture in sophisticated Danish design. This is, so to speak, the commercial antithesis of the design museum, because here, of course, you can buy all the items. For a long time I wanted to buy an original Louis Poulsen lamp. And later I did. However, I bought the good piece, the "PH 5", second-hand - which can be worthwhile with original design items.

Now we undertake the contrast programme to the city centre: we pay a visit to Christiania. But we don't go to the area where the ships are moored on the canals, but further south. The "Free City of Christiania" has developed from an autonomous municipality into a Copenhagen attraction of the first order. "Christiania was founded in 1971 when a group of squatters cut a hole in the fence to the military barracks in Bådmandsgade," the tourist information brochure tells us. This area became known as

"Pusher Street", where you could buy "soft" drugs. Many of the original residents have remained in the settlement to this day, which is collectively run. Some houses are self-built, there are restaurants and galleries. In 2012, the "Christiania" foundation managed to pay the Danish state a considerable sum by issuing "people's shares" so that it could continue to dispose of the site itself.

The people seem relaxed, quite different from the busy city centre. We stroll criss-cross through the neighbourhood. I find it quite original. The residents are not so closed off. We walk purposefully through the alleys and don't try to "out" ourselves as tourists. When we ask or order something, we are always treated in a friendly way.

Perhaps the secret of Christiania is that the neighbourhood has been more successful in resisting the "gentrification" that is spreading in Hamburg's Schanzenviertel or in Berlin's Kreuzberg and Friedrichshain. More and more visitors and tourists come, fancier bars move in and eventually expensive new buildings are erected, into which wealthy people move who want to partici-pate in the "trendy" structure of the neighbourhoods and yet displace them themselves. In Christiania this seems impossible, precisely because of the self-government of the neighbourhood. Visitors who want to learn even more are recommended to join one of the city tours, where "local guides" take walks through the neighbourhood and provide background information.

On our shore excursion through Copenhagen, we now arrive back in Nyhavn, the former bustling trading port where ships from all over the world once docked and sailors frequented the pubs. Today the old houses are all finely renovated and restau-rants dominate. This is the opposite of Christiania: here the tourists are still real tourists who appear in noisy groups. But Nyhavn is also known as the "Port of Hans Christian Andersen". For the famous writer, who came from Odense, lived in house no. 20 for a time and wrote some fairy tales there. Andersen also lived at No. 67, supposedly for 20 years, and for two more years at No. 18. From Nyhavn, we take one of the water taxis that run on the river like a regular bus, and drive the short distance back to Langelinie. On the way, we pass "The Royal Theatre", Copenhagen's new opera house. The house with its modern architecture is a donation from the foundation "A.P. Møller and Chastine Mc-Kinney Møller". This is the company of the founder of the shipping company Maersk, which today is the largest company in Scandinavia. The 1400-seat building was completed in 2005 and has since received several architectural awards.

The statue of the Little Mermaid in Copenhagen by the water

In friendly Copenhagen, visitors can spend days and spend time at many attractions. "Nyhavn", for example, was only two kilometres away from our "Langelinie Lystbådehavn", always along the water. After two days, we cast off our lines and set sail again. On a somewhat rainy but windy day in July, we made the small "hop" to an island in the middle of the Öresund: the "Flakfortet". It was just 5.15 nautical miles, but you have to sail around the massive wind farm that lies just outside the harbour exit of Copenhagen.

The fort is another world. It is located on the artificial island "Saltholmrev" and was built between 1910 and 1914 to complete the defence of Copenhagen from the sea side. Initially, 550 soldiers were stationed on the island, which is only 0.3 square kilometres in size, and they had to operate a number of larger guns. It was not until 1975 that the Ministry of Defence leased the fort to the Copenhagen Sailing Association, so that civilians could now also moor here. The great sheltered harbour lies behind the breakwater, which forms a ring around the fort inside. In 2001, the site was sold to the private Swedish company "Malmökranen", which has since run the marina, the restaurant, the museum and a small hotel. Up to 200 boats can be accommodated there, but at about 30 euros per night (with a boat length of up to 12 metres) it is not a cheap pleasure, but not an expensive one either, when you think of the Danish price level. In return, there are all the necessary facilities and you can roam the fort's grounds into the night and admire the lights on both sides of the Öresund. This is a historical gem in the middle of the water.

From "Flakfortet" it was not far to Malmö. The Swedish city is a good ten nautical miles away. You sail past the island of Saltholmen in the north and then set a direct course for Malmö harbour. Before the Öresund Bridge was built, ferries used to sail here in close succession, connecting the two cities. We also spent some wonderful days in Malmö. Of course, the city is smaller than Copenhagen, but it is also worth a visit. But now back to the southern exit of the Öresund and back to the sailing trip from Haparanda to Hamburg.

17 FROM DENMARK TO HAMBURG

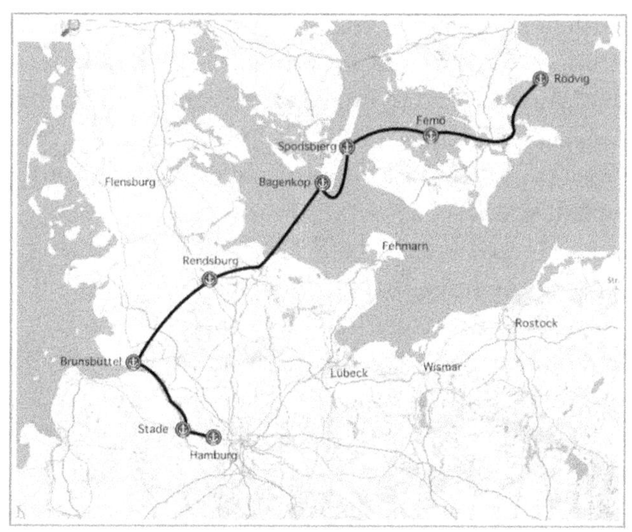

Whoever sails up here, at the southern end of the Öresund, and wants to get to central Europe, especially Hamburg, finds himself in a convenient location. Because again there are three ways for the last part of the journey. On the way here we used the Kiel Canal and then sailed north via Fehmarn. Now we could keep a course south and sail to Lübeck, then use the canal to the Elbe with the mast laid down.

Or, and this seems to me the most attractive way, one sails into the Storstrømmen. This runs between the main Danish island of Zealand and the island of Mön, later passing the northern side of Lolland and Falster. It flows into the Smålandsfarvandet, the Smalands fairway. Some places are suitable for a stopover, as there are pretty islands. You could say that if you were to write a book about sailing in the Danish South Seas, you would certainly recommend the Smaland waterway.

I am looking forward to crossing the familiar waters and set off for the island of Femø, 46 nautical miles away. With a fresh wind, I cross the Faxe Bugt into the narrow but well-buoyed fairway at full speed.

I leave the large harbours of Kalvehave and Vordingborg to starboard, pass the large bridge over the Storstrømmen and the construction site for the new railway bridge, which will one day connect Hamburg with Copenhagen via the Belt Tunnel. Only then can "Svanen" sail around the island of Femø in the north and enter the harbour. Here I once fought my way into the port many years ago with the Kelt 620 under outboard motor with a sound wave. I could still find space in the farthest corner in the crowded harbour with the small boat.

Evening atmosphere in Spodsbjerg before the storm approaches

This worry does not exist today: I have never experienced this harbour as empty as now. Here is clearly the free choice of place. This is not much different the next day when I moor in Spodsbjerg on Langeland. There is still a camping site with a snack bar, but the excellent supermarket in the village has been closed for a long time. The many fishing boats in the harbour are interesting, which are advertised for charter. They are ready for visitors, who make ample use of them in this calm weather and try their luck fishing in the Great Belt.

Unfortunately, the weather is now changing, as the forecast unmistakably announces. The comparatively calm late summer weather is replaced by rain and a lot of wind. I manage to leave the harbour exit of Spodsbjerg the next day, hoist the reefed mainsail and unfurl the genoa halfway. But at the same time, gusts of 24 knots, that is force six, whistle across the Great Belt from the east. Really nasty waves are building up, which I fear could shake the boat. But that does not happen: "Svanen" is relatively stable on the wind on her course to the south and makes good speed. The rain comes from the front. The drops slap on the spray hood, but on the other hand, you can squeeze behind the cloth, keep a lookout and not get too wet. The visibility is poor. Other boats are only late to recognise through the rain.

And then it happens: A loud bang comes from the mast, and before I know it, the mainsail collapses. I have no explanation for the first few seconds and look around in horror. Then I see that the main halyard has snapped. A short stub is all that is left of the halyard that holds the sail up. The rope is 12 millimetres thick, and actually, it still looked usable - but here, it could no longer withstand the strain. It's just as well that the autopilot continues to steer cleanly, while the reefed genoa alone can drive "Svanen" forward. I go leashed to the forecastle and fold up the wet cloth, which I tie to the boom. Too bad, I think. We already have the route from Finland in the wake, and then the main halyard breaks shortly before Langeland. It is absolutely clear that I head for the next harbour, Bagenkop, at the southern tip of Langeland. As if to confirm that the Baltic Sea can't be without risks here either, a yacht washed up on the beach appears to starboard. The ship lies diagonally on the land, looking like a sad wreck. I'm creeped out by these conditions: Wind force six onshore, heavy rain and no more main halyard.

In front of Bagenkop, there is a crowd. Almost like a zipper, the yachts sail into the harbour. I take down the sails and steer carefully towards the pier heads when a brand new dark blue Bavaria yacht thinks she has to push in front of "Svanen" with full sails. It looks as if the berths are about to run out. What's up with the skipper? I don't know. Directly in front of my bow, the crew calmly takes down the sails in the harbour entrance and doesn't care about other ships. You could call that an impressive manoeuvre in disregard of good seamanship.

But a little later, when "Svanen" has long since been well

moored at a jetty, the strange spectacle of Bagenkop continues. Essentially, it always follows the same pattern: a large, reasonably new yacht, presumably a charter ship, comes into the harbour basin. A nervous skipper yells commands, the crew runs around excitedly. The bow thruster growls, and then there is a bang as the ship hits the harbour wall. This spectacle is repeated five times throughout the evening until a small Danish yacht crashes right into "Svanen's" starboard side.

But nothing happened. The thick fenders on both ships prevented it. A young Danish couple apologises profusely for not keeping their brightly painted vessel under control. I say you can hardly blame them for that either, in this weather. "Yeah, and it's our first trip on the boat. We're really unlucky with the weather," says the young skipper. I'm happy to help them tie up. Shortly afterwards, another huge charter yacht drifts uncontrollably through the harbour basin. She lies down at the very end of the dock between the small fishing boats, which looks quite strange.

Indeed, there is a wind force six, and the conditions in the harbour are really not easy. But one would like to call out to some skippers: Take it easy for once. Sail gently in the port and don't shout nervous commands. And look for a comfortable berth and head for it in peace. All this hectic mooring will get you nowhere. Even if you overdo it a little with the calm, what's the big deal? A couple on a fancy modern yacht drives for half an hour through the whole harbour basin with all the rows of boxes before they are pretty sure that they have chosen the right place - which they then navigate unerringly. They certainly had less stress in the process.

The wind still rushes over Langeland for a few days. The mainsail I have helpfully repaired: I could pull a spare line through the mast. For this, I used the dirk, which is the line that holds the boom when no sail is set, and which also runs through the mast and is led out of the masthead aft. The only difference is that now the main halyard comes out of the mast on the port side, so you have to rethink it a bit.

A break due to bad weather in Bagenkop

I try it, leave the harbour and set course southwest with reefed sails. The ship is difficult to steer because the sails are not properly balanced in the reef. But with the waves, I don't have the breath to climb onto the forecastle and tie in the second reef, especially as the ride could still become very uncomfortable afterwards: It's too choppy out there for me. The waves coming from the south are too high, slowing down the journey considerably. I'm back on the same jetty a little later, just a little further towards land. I prefer to wait before I tackle the next stroke.

And on Langeland, a visit to the main town of Rudkøbing is a good idea, located in the middle of the long island and easily reached by bus from Bagenkop in half an hour. Of course, you have to buy tickets electronically in advance here too, but unlike Sweden, you don't need to install your own app. And Rudkøbing has a friendly pedestrian zone with pretty shops to offer.

Nevertheless, I confess that certain restlessness arises again: The schedule is tight. Isn't it now time to "make distance"? That's what goes through my mind while "Svanen" lies in her last Danish port on this trip. But no, I have just deviated from that motto myself. I'd rather turn back trying than take unnecessary risks. I go over my itinerary and find that there is still plenty of time to make the return trip before the end of September. I just didn't think that a forced break would occur so close to the German coast. When the wind has finally calmed down, the whitecaps in front of the harbour have disappeared, the sun comes through again a little, "Svanen" sets off towards Germany. The southern tip of Langeland slowly disappears on the horizon. Shortly before the sea border, I notice a boat from the Danish coast guard, which is heading strangely exact to "Svanen". Does he really want to come to me, I ask myself?

Well, I see no reason to slow down until he makes a statement. But there's nothing but static on the radio. And because I don't take the speed out, I'm quickly over the sea line, too. The coastguard boat stays behind and takes up a position precisely on the line representing the border on the sea chart. It will probably be waiting there for "customers" who might be worth checking out.

After passing the Bülk lighthouse, the traffic becomes heavier again, but the way to the Kiel Canal is not far. In one go, I enter the lock chamber, which fortunately has just opened for pleasure boats, and shortly afterwards, the gates close. Now "Svanen" is safe for the time being, I think, at least from rugged seas and annoying gusts. Behind the lock, there is the yacht yard Dick, where we already had our boat in winter storage, which is very recommendable. Of all the winter storage facilities where we have stored our boats, i.e. in Hamburg, Berlin and Bremerhaven, this one on the canal was one of the best.

But now we have the trip through the channel ahead of us, which could require many hours of patience. But I don't feel that way. After the stormy experiences of the past days, I find the quiet ride quite comfortable. Above all, co-skipper Birgit is on board again, which makes the last part of the way to Hamburg much more pleasant. Via Rendsburg we head for Brunsbüttel, where we moor in the harbour on the inland side of the locks.

Stopover in Rendsburg in northern Germany

It is actually always full here, even in autumn. The moorings fill up into the evening. Some boats lie crammed next to each other. I am glad to finally meet a stern buoy at the end of the harbour basin, which I have in best memory. Zack, the buoy hook sits and "Svanen" is moored safely. The masks worn everywhere in the small town centre of Brunsbüttel take some getting used to again, after so many maskless weeks in Sweden and Denmark. Now the River Elbe is coming up again. The tide calendar is well disposed towards us: Around 11 o'clock is low water the following day, then the tidal wave runs up the river.

We get through the lock without much delay. The first thing I notice is the grey water of the Elbe. That is quite a contrast to the blue waters of the Baltic Sea. But on the coast between Hamburg and Frisia, the water is always grey from the sand it carries. Further out, however, it's as clear as in the Swedish archipelago.

We sail comfortably with the tide up the river and let ourselves be pushed hard. "Svanen" is approaching Hamburg with the tide at a speed of eight knots. I can't resist and put Hans Albers on the little Bluetooth box in the cockpit. "The Elbe, the Michel, the course is always good," sings "blond Hans", while "Svanen" cruises upstream, keeping a reasonable distance from commercial shipping.

I find it amazing how well we are on schedule in the end. Despite all the obstacles, such as the bad weather before Bagenkop or beforehand at Mariehamn, and despite the many ports, the schedule works out well. This has to be celebrated. And therefore, we decide to make a stopover in a city close to the Elbe. We treat ourselves to a two-day detour to Stade. For this purpose, we go up the little river Schwinge, directly into the old town. Here, too, in the pretty harbour basin, we have to get used to low tide again. "Svanen" lies at a floating jetty and "rides" up and down with the tide. Just now, she is almost at the level of the quay edge. Six hours later, she sinks into the silt lying on the bottom of the harbour basin. There are no significant tidal differences in the Baltic Sea.

Nevertheless, coming home after this long journey is especially nice. Upstream from Stade, we pass the island Lühesand before setting course for the marina Wedel next to Neßsand. Soon the Vindö comes into her winter storage, so the first way leads us to the gas station to fill up the diesel tank for the winter. This is to prevent condensation from forming on the inside of the tank. As "Svanen" hangs on the hook a few days later and floats into storage, wistfulness might set in. After such a trip we have to take a break from sailing in autumn. But we have come a long way: The way back from Stockholm to Hamburg alone was 621.2 nautical miles long, corresponding to 1150 kilometres.

And the conclusion of the whole trip? From Hamburg to Haparanda and back, we have covered 2387 nautical miles - that's precisely 4421 kilometres. A respectable distance, especially since we are not sailing a huge yacht, but a boat with nine meters in length. But this boat has what it takes, as shown on the journey. The long keeler can be steered well through choppy seas and completes many manoeuvres calmly and stably, such as berthing in choppy seas, which is more difficult in a modern short keeler.

Since the spring of 1980 "Svanen" has been sailing on the Baltic Sea. She had owners in Middelfahrt in Denmark, in Dragör near Copenhagen and in Faxe Ladeplads in Faxe Bugt, who have lovingly cared for the ship over all these years. In the harbours where she was moored, she always cut a wonderful figure with her unmistakable mahogany superstructure - unless another Vindö was lying next to her, of course. But now she has once sailed to the end of the Baltic Sea, respectively, the Gulf of Bothnia. There has been no real damage to our older but well-maintained Vindö, apart from the cracked main halyard. The lesson to be learned from this is: before a more extended trip, check the standing and running rigging, i.e. the shrouds, the halyards and the sheets. And if in doubt, replace them.

The ship and the equipment are much more stressed on a longer trip than on a shorter holiday trip or a weekend trip on the Baltic Sea. But the mast has withstood all stresses without any problems, the diesel has never let us down, the rudder has always kept the ship on course. Neither the heating nor the cooker failed, the defect in the water pump was quickly repaired. At most, I would advise against installing a do-it-yourself navigation system and prefer a chart plotter that can still be operated without any problems, even in rough seas. But otherwise, even the older navigation instruments provided reliable data: This includes speeds over ground and through the water, depth, heading, and of course wind direction and speed.

At home: "Svanen" on the quay in Stade, just outside Hamburg

Maybe we would make the beds a little more comfortable, after a few weeks the hard support is not comfortable on your back. Before we could set sail for new destinations again, work is pending. By the way, the antifouling on the hull has held up excellently. No pox or shells have settled on the underwater hull. This is simply because the ship has been in motion a lot. In addition, the mahogany deck structure on the Vindö needs to be sanded down and repainted so that the wood will have adequate UV protection again next summer. I will rearrange the wiring harnesses. After all, I want to have the lights ready at the push of a button and not improvise. The sails are already at a sailmaker, who will repair the cracks.

Cruising is indeed a unique way to travel, as this trip has

shown - which is only representative of many possible trips along the coasts of Europe. It is incomparable to sail to islands, harbours and cities in Scandinavia. No matter whether you choose Haparanda as your destination or explore the Baltic Sea further south. No matter whether you travel via Sweden or the Baltic States: a trip to the Bothnian Sea is full of variety. It is comfortable because the route leads along the coast in longer sections.

You will encounter exciting harbours with friendly and helpful people, beautiful archipelago waters and large, exciting cities. And - who knows - maybe you get to see Mr Moose, not only on land but swimming between the beautiful islands of the archipelagos. We will sure come back looking for him.

18 BONUS CHAPTER: HAMBURG

In front of us lies the Lower Elbe ("Unterelbe"), the shipping route that leads from the North Sea to the port of Hamburg. So it makes sense to visit the city on a trip to Scandinavia. From Cuxhaven or Brunsbüttel, where the Kiel Canal has its western exit at the lock gates, it would only take seven to eight hours at rising water to reach the city by boat.

There are a number of larger vessels anchored off Brunsbüttel, waiting to enter the canal. There is also a throng of pleasure boats floating in front of the canal entrance, set against the current. It looks reasonably peaceful in this calm weather. But it's hard to imagine what it's like in stormy seas - the entrance to the canal locks seems quite unprotected, and the "waiting places for pleasure boats" are in the middle of the river in front of it. On the other hand, the whole area is still somewhat sheltered from the vagaries of the North Sea, and the many sandbanks in the Elbe estuary will probably keep the larger waves out even in bad weather.

Many ships pass the leisure sailors here. I still remember well how a container freighter from Hapag-Lloyd passed us, which already had a lot of speed out here. Its wake shook us up quite a bit. But everything important stays in its place in the cabin. Still, I got a fright: So the container giants aren't so peaceful after all, it's a matter of keeping as much distance as possible from them.

When the weather is nice, there is a great harbour up here, in Otterndorf, on the other side of the Elbe. Here the Medem River flows into the Elbe, separated by a barrage. The "Hadelner Canal", also known as the "Elbe Weser Shipping Route", arrives in Otterndorf. This connects the village with Bremerhaven and can be a nice alternative to sailing on the North Sea if you want to enter the Weser. However, a grim lock-keeper "guards" the exit of the canal at the Otterndorf lock, and you should beware of him. He grumbles a lot about yachts that don't respect the strict speed limit on the canal. After all, a new, large lock has been built here. But with a mast, there is no way through for sailing yachts on the low bridges of the canal.

Birgit wanted to be sure and had called the harbour master to clarify the situation: In Otterndorf, when the tide is out, you can sink into the soft silt of the Elbe. And the friendly harbour master had assured her that this should not be a problem for our boat with its draught of 1.30 metres.

We take a walk to the mouth of the Medem River at the Elbe. It is wonderfully fresh out here: the view goes far to the other side of the Elbe, which almost disappears on the horizon. And you can walk on to a holiday settlement where a small bathing lake has been built - probably quite useful in case high and low tide don't play along when it comes to swimming. Upstream, on the Medem, after about 2.5 kilometres, you come to the small town of Otterndorf with its pretty little houses and the large church, St. Severin's Church, also known as "Bauerndom". This evening, however, we visit the restaurant close to the harbour with its beautiful view of the large container ships that sail ceaselessly up and down the Elbe.

After the „matjes", what else should I have ordered here in style, we head back to our boat. The water has almost completely drained away, there seem to be only puddles between the moorings. But the yacht is lying upright. As I step onto the boat, I notice that it is not swaying a bit. In fact: the keel has bored into the silt, the ship is now on the bottom and no longer floating in the water.

Here you get a nice view of the Lower Elbe landscape and towns to the left and right of the Elbe river. I would be only too tempted to go up the Oste, the river that flows into the Elbe a little before the Medem. Theoretically, it's even navigable as far as Bremervörde.

I'm thinking of a little swim before setting off. The water is still shallow, I notice, but deep enough to swim in. And it seems to be salt water that is being printed there by the tide into the mouth of the Elbe and then flowed up the Medem into the harbour. So the water must be all right, too. As a Hamburger, one always has reservations about bathing in the Elbe. This river is used as a shipping route and for industry, it's not bathing water, it goes through my head. Bathing? Hamburgers would do that at most on the beach of St. Peter-Ording in the North Sea. But the risk in the city is mainly due to the current, not so much to the water quality.

Out here in the Medem, just before the mouth of the Elbe, you really don't have to worry. The swim is refreshing, given the muggy heat that hangs over the harbour when we were there.

There is enough room to sail out here on the Elbe, even if you have to cross. Towards Hamburg, the river narrows. A nice stopover on the way to the Hanseatic city is Glückstadt. We chug leisurely around the harbour head and look for a place in the outer harbour in front of the barrage where we can moor the boat. It's nice out here. The only disadvantage is that the sanitary facilities are a short walk away, as you have to walk across the barrage first.

By the way, this is the home of an interesting type of boat: high-quality yachts came from the shipyard "Asmus KG Yacht-bau", founded by master carpenter Willy Asmus in 1965. Asmus yachts were built here until 1990: 378 in 16 different designs. The

"Hanseat 70" was particularly popular, with 200 of them being laid down.

Glückstadt also has an interesting history: the Danish King Christian IV founded "Lykstadt" in 1617 to compete with Hamburg. However, the pretty little town has stood still somewhat in time: As a port, Glückstadt has never been able to develop much. And as a suburb for commuters, it is already too far from Hamburg, even though the Marschenbahn railway runs along here from the west coast. The inland harbour behind the lock is really beautiful and so are the numerous old houses that line it. It's just part of it now: once again I order matjes in a small restaurant with a garden at the harbour, because Glückstadt is probably famous for its matjes (which here, as elsewhere, has of course long since come from Holland).

From Glückstadt it's not far to Hamburg. Hamburg's maritime centre is the edge of the harbour, which stretches from the "fish market" via the "Landungsbrücken" to the new Hafencity district. You can stroll along the whole stretch on a developed promenade. Certainly, at the "Landungsbrücken" it becomes very touristy: souvenir shops crowd next to snack stalls, in between coaches spit out their guests who then hurry to the harbour tours. But that, too, is part of Germany's second-largest city with its more than 1.8 million inhabitants. Hamburg is fond of water. You can see this in the city centre, which borders the large lake "Alster" at Jungfernstieg, where sailors in small boats are out and about, rowers, canoeists and the white "Alster steamers". There is a nice contrast between these two places: here the large harbour with its ships, shipyards and ferries and a rather rough charm. There the thoroughly fine lake with its water sports enthusiasts. And in between is the city centre with its shopping streets and commercial buildings.

The river Elbe in front of the container terminal

If you come to Hamburg via the Elbe, you can choose between three harbours. There are perhaps not quite as many berths as in Copenhagen or Stockholm, but the Elbe is also a somewhat more complicated sailing area than the calm Scandinavian waters. This is partly due to the tide, of course, as we learned at the beginning of the book near Cuxhaven. You will need the tide tables to sail up the river to Hamburg with rising water if possible. The outgoing water is shorter, by the way: a stopover will be unavoidable for a sailing boat going down the Elbe to the North Sea to wait for the time between two tides.

But when we have made it and the suburb of Wedel appears on the port side behind the town of Stade on starboard, the first marina is also just around the corner, the enormous "Hamburg marina in Wedel". The facility at the gates of the city is very spacious: there are almost 2000 berths there, on floating pontoons that lower with the tide. So you can moor there regardless of the tide, just like in the other two harbours. In keeping with the many boats, there is also a wide range of nautical services: There are repair shops, sailmakers, a nice pub and all the facilities that characterise a good harbour, such as a gas station. The good news: it's not expensive to moor there either, the prices are moderate. Now comes the downside: you are far out from the city, which is just beginning here. You would miss the trip to the harbour, the banks of the Elbe suburbs with their green hills on the northern edge of the Elbe, the busy container terminals in Waltershof, the harbour edge in Altona. A suburban railway runs into the city from Wedel. However, you have to walk or take a taxi to the station, as there is no bus from the harbour. Good luck to those who have managed to fit an on-board bicycle on their boat. The "S-Bahn" takes you to the "Landungsbrücken" or straight to the "Jungfernstieg" station in the centre.

If you continue on the Elbe and leave Wedel on your port side, you will pass the pretty, spruced-up Elbe suburb of Blankenese after a few nautical miles, then the large Airbus aircraft factory follows on your starboard side. Directly behind the runway, the small "Rüschkanal" branches off from the Elbe in the district of "Finkenwerder". And there you will find a whole series of marinas run by clubs and two shipyards. There are many berths for guests here. They are as different as the club they belong to. But in the forest of sailing boat masts that awaits you here, you are sure to find a nice spot. It's not expensive here either. The only catch is - you'll have guessed it already: the connection to the centre. This time, however, there is a bus stop from where you can take the bus to Altona, a district on the other side of the Elbe. It goes through the Elbe tunnel, where a large north-south motorway has been built under the river. Even more charming is the walk from the Rüschkanal through a park to the Elbe and take a ferry that goes into the city to the "Landungsbrücken". Either take the ferry from the "Rüschpark" pier to Finkenwerder and change there, or walk straight to the Finkenwerder pier.

If you continue on the Elbe, you have to pay particular attention now, because it's getting crowded in the harbour. Small cargo ships, excursion steamers, the harbour ferries and the occasional large ship come from all sides, because now we pass the container terminals. Instead, the absolute top attraction for water sports enthusiasts lies ahead of us: the "City Sportboothafen" at Baumwall. This modern, well-kept harbour is to Hamburg what the "Wasahamn" is to Stockholm or "St. Katherin's Dock" is to London. And although it is more expensive than the other two Hamburg ports, it does not yet reach the prices of the Scandinavian capitals or London. So if you make it through the hustle and bustle of boats and ferries in the harbour, you can turn to port and make a nice curve into the harbour. The entrance is well shown on the nautical charts, it is deep enough everywhere here, even at low tide.

The floating jetties are wide and have enough possibilities to moor the boat. Call the harbour master beforehand and he can assign you a place (or tell you if everything is occupied, because this harbour is not that huge). Now you would have a place in the middle of the city, between the Landungsbrücken and the modern Hafencity. There is electricity, water, sanitary facilities - in fact, everything that goes with it. The waterfront is only a few metres away via a (steep) bridge. I would have loved to station our boat here, but the harbour is for guests visiting Hamburg. That doesn't stop us from mooring here ourselves occasionally, that's how beautiful I find the place.

Our yacht with the mast laid down in the „City Sportboothafen"

Hamburg is a pleasant big city. And many Hamburgers are proud of their harbour and of the city's maritime past, which was independent for centuries and belonged neither to Prussia nor to Denmark. In the 1850s, people were particularly fond of Great Britain and the saying "When it rains in London, they open their umbrellas in Hamburg" dates back to that time - which is supposed to illustrate how much Hamburg looked to the British island and its capital. Whether Hamburg still seems particularly British today, I leave to your judgement. But there are still some connections today, such as the fine "Anglo German Club" on the Alster: after the inglorious Second World War, the Deputy Regional Commissioner of the British Military Government wanted to use a villa to found a club. This was to work to put relations with Great Britain back on a friendly footing. The club became a success because it was also supported by many politicians from Hamburg.

To this day, it hosts events such as dinners with English and German guests from politics, business and culture, an annual golf tournament, Christmas dinners and the Garden Party. The club also supports institutions such as the Anglican Church of England in Hamburg, the "Church of St Thomas Becket", which is located not far from St Michaelis Church, the "Michel". This magnificent main church is well worth a visit.

How would you now conquer the city from the edge of the harbour, whether you came by ferry from Finkenwerder, by train from Wedel or simply walked a few metres from the "City Sportboothafen"? The centre at Jungfernstieg is only a 20-minute walk away. From Baumwall, keep to the right for a few hundred metres until you come to the mouth of a canal, the "Alsterfleet". Then turn left along the street next to the canal, which is called "Am Alsterfleet". Behind a large hotel, the "Steigenberger", the centre already follows with its shopping arcades and the street "Neuer Wall", where there are already many, rather high-priced shops. From Jungfernstieg you can walk west towards Gänsemarkt, or east towards "Mönkebergstraße" with department stores (the last ones left) and many large shops belonging to chains.

What else should visitors to the city not miss? There is the famous "Reeperbahn", an amusement mile in the west of the city, close to the edge of the harbour. This is a very lively amusement district that harks back to Hamburg's old seafaring tradition. Certainly, you will find a number of tourist traps, amusement arcades, dance halls „of the lowest drawer", as they say in German. Especially on weekend nights, the "Reeperbahn" almost collapses from the throng of amusement-seeking tourists who haunt the red-light district. But there are also good music clubs, like the "Docks" at Spielbudenplatz, or the "Große Freiheit 36" in a side street. Incidentally, this is where the "Beatles" arrived from Liverpool in the 1960s and gave concerts before they had their breakthrough. On 17 August 1960, they stood on a stage in Hamburg for the first time, in a club opposite "Große Freiheit 36", which unfortunately no longer exists. On the other hand, there are some original pubs in the side streets of the "Reeperbahn" that can be worth a visit. Only the sailors from the big cargo ships on their shore leave, you won't find them here anymore: The time the freighters spend in port is too short and the quays are too far away from the entertainment district for the crews to afford to come to St. Pauli.

If this is too touristy for you, we recommend a visit to the "Schanzenviertel" around the street "Schulterblatt". It's also a bit rowdy, but not quite as touristy as the Reeperbahn. You can find some good pubs on Schulterblatt. Much more dignified would be a visit to districts like Eppendorf, Hoheluft or Winterhude, which are grouped around the Alster in the north and are affluent, inner-city neighbourhoods. Only in Hamburg's city centre, there is hardly anything to do after office hours. When the shops are closed in the evening, the centre seems deserted. A stroll through Hafencity, where there are now also many bars and restaurants, is more advisable. This new district on the edge of the Elbe has been under development since the 1980s. It is an urban development project like those in many port cities around the world (Bremen also has its Überseequartier, for example). Not as big as London's Docklands, Hafencity has an interesting, very modern architecture. Its highlight is the renowned concert hall "Elbphilharmonie". You can see it towering from afar on the edge of the harbour. It is only a short walk from the "City Sportboothafen". Perhaps a visit to the city can be combined with a visit to the "Elbphilharmonie"? From the observation terrace in the old warehouse on the Elbe, you have a very nice overview of the city and the harbour.

There are a lot of sailors in Hamburg. No statistics are kept on exactly how many there are. That would be a field for market researchers who deal with the target group of sailors. But the German Sailing Association (DSV) has 70 member clubs in the Hanseatic city. There are 103 in Berlin and 31 in Bremen. Sailors are very present in Hamburg's cityscape, namely on the Alster. People like to sail a lot right in the centre.

But you can't just sail your boat onto the Alster and set sail there, as you could in Berlin on the Wannsee, for example. First of all, anyone can sail, paddle or row on the Alster without official permission. An official permit is required for sailing with "machine-driven vehicles". Even a larger sailing yacht would belong to this if it travels under motor through the canals that lead from the Elbe to the Alster in the city centre. The permit would be required at the latest when a yacht enters the Alster through the Rathausschleuse.

The competent environmental authority states that "official approval may be granted subject to conditions and requirements". In officialese, "may be given" is a forewarning that there will most likely be no permit. So you should have an impeccable reason why you want to take your boat onto the Alster. The Alster is a recreational area where motorboats are not allowed. If you are visiting Hamburg and would like to sail on the Alster, there are a number of rental companies where you can hire a sailing boat - from "Bobby Reich" in the north at Krugkoppelbrücke to "Segelschule Pieper" in the south. And then you can experience for yourself the mixture of sudden downdrafts and lots of sailboat traffic, coupled with fast Alster steamers, that the lake in the middle of the city offers recreational skippers. Nevertheless, it is a wonderful experience to glide across the Alster in a small keelboat or a dinghy.

By the way, there is a very special jetty at "Bobby Reich": here lies a considerable fleet of Conger-type dinghies, like the one we own ourselves. This was once built at the "Blohm + Voss" shipyard in Hamburg and is still very popular on the Alster. I had once considered putting the Conger on the Alster, and a good offer was made to me at "Bobby Reich". For the time being, however, the dinghy will remain on an inland lake north of Hamburg. Would you like to rent it? One or two people pay 22 euros an hour and can then cruise on the Alster.

Sailing on the Elbe is, of course, a tradition in Hamburg. Not just as a recreational sport, as it is today. The whole history of the port of Hamburg revolves around the sailing ships that sailed here for hundreds of years. Sailing was pure necessity if you wanted to trade in goods. As early as the 9th century, a wooden jetty was erected on an island in the Elbe, where ships could moor. The heyday came after 1375, when trade increased more and more in the following years and the city's population doubled to 16,000 in 75 years. And it was always small sailing ships that sailed up and down the Elbe and travelled the North Sea. The era of cargo ships under sail lasted until 1957, ending with the "Pamir".

The era of yachting goes back as far as 1661, when the first documented regatta of sailing boats took place in England. The oldest sailing club in Germany that still exists today is the "Segel-club Rhe", which was founded as early as 1855 in Königsberg and is now based in Hamburg. With the founding of the German Sailing Association (DSV) in 1888, the enthusiasm for yacht sailing finally spilled over from England and the USA to Germany, including the Elbe. Here, the North German Regatta Association (NRV), founded as early as 1868, recorded steady growth. "Hamburg merchants with foreign contacts and Britons in Hamburg had brought gentleman's rowing and pleasure sailing to the Free and Hanseatic City from around 1840," writes the NRV in its chronicle. "The new water sports were very British in origin and quickly became very Hanseatic on the Alster and Elbe." And even today, this club is still one of the largest and best-known in Germany.

Is there now a typical boat for the Elbe? Yes, of course. For example, there is the "Elb-H-Jolle", a real classic that was constructed over 70 years ago. "The Elb-H-Jolle was developed for the conditions prevailing on the Elbe," writes the class association for this type of boat. Because there is often a lot of wind and the tide causes steep waves. "The freeboard and the length-to-width ratio are perfectly suited to the area." The pretty, gaff-rigged H-yachts are indeed seen more often on the Elbe. And the "Conger", which for many belongs on the Alster, can also be called an Elbe dinghy. It is robust and can be fitted with a small outboard motor at the stern. But above all, the Conger was developed on the Elbe, with test runs in the Mühlenberger Loch. That makes it an Elbe dinghy, too, in my opinion.

When we leave the marina at Baumwall by boat once again and head down the Elbe, we pass the Altona fish market. From the water, the modern buildings look even higher than from the land, I think. The terminal of the former England Ferry comes into view. What times were those when a ferry from Hamburg to Harwich left here several times a week before the low-cost airlines put an end to it. At first, the shipping company let it continue to sail from Cuxhaven for a while, only to turn off the juice to the loss-making company at the end of the 1990s. It's a pity, so there is no longer a regular passenger service from Hamburg to England, even though some of the older postcards sold at the landing stages still show the ship on the Elbe.

The museum harbour Övelgönne is passed to starboard. My heart sinks: How often have I looked out over the water from this beautiful harbour, with its small but fine selection of old ships? On the port side, it becomes a bit monotonous at the Bubendey bank, here are storage tanks of an oil refinery. But on starboard, the slopes of the Elbe suburbs now tower up. Here are truly magnificent villas, bordered on the "wet side" by the Elbe, to the rear by the boulevard Elbchaussee. Then comes Teufelsbrück with its small marina and, on the other side, Finkenwerder.

On the north side of the river, the Nienstedten church comes into view, the traditional Louis C. Jacobs on the slopes of the Elbe and then we approach Blankenese.

The suburb's ferry terminal is exactly six nautical miles from Hamburg's Landungsbrücken. But there is no longer a direct connection. But there is still a small ferry that you can take from Blankenese to Teufelsbrück.

Blankenese is still an exciting place today, despite the fame it has gained as a wealthy suburb in Hamburg's west. This is because life here takes place between the banks of the Elbe and the Geestrücken ridge that stretches high above the Elbe. This is where the Blankeneser Treppenviertel is located: countless small and larger houses nestle against the Elbe slope, which is criss-crossed by small streets and pedestrian paths. At the bottom is the ferry dock, the "Bulln", so called because cattle used to be driven ashore here. And then steep stairs lead up to "Sagebiel's Ferry House", which has been around since the 19th century and stands about halfway up the hill. From there, you continue up the stairs to the top. You can then stroll along Blankeneser Bahn-hofstraße, which is lined with numerous shops, to reach the S-Bahn station. If you don't like climbing so many stairs, you can take one of the "mountain goats", which are the minibuses that have been going from Strandweg to the town for decades.

It's just a pity that Blankenese doesn't have its own marina. Where do the people of Blankenese leave their boats? The old local chronicle describes how the Elbe beaches off Blankenese were full of buoys a hundred years ago. There, the sailing boats lay close together, regardless of the current of the tide. Today that is no longer the case. Wait a minute, many die-hard Blankenese residents will now interject, we do have the "BSC". Yes, that's right, and Birgit and I once studied for our German sailing licence, the Sportbootführerschein See, at the Blankeneser Segel-club. It is located at the eastern end of Strandweg and has a small "Blankeneser Jollenhafen". On it floats a pontoon with the club-house and an excellent, sturdy restaurant. But it is only a small harbour with a handful of berths, and at low tide large parts of it also dry out. We refrain from mooring there when the water is running out, even though it is a pity that we cannot visit Blanke-nese so easily by boat. This district has always lived with and from the Elbe, even in the days a few hundred years ago when it was still a fishing village on the slopes of the river.

Diagonally opposite, on the other side of the Elbe, lies "the"

Blankenes sailing area. Excuse me, that's actually where the Blankeneser Revier was. Because a good part of it has been built over in the meantime: The Mühlenberger Loch was filled in with sand over an area of 160 hectares from 2001 to 2003. This is the site of the expanded Airbus plant in Hamburg, which was prepared for the production of the giant A 380 - although this aircraft is now history again, as it is no longer manufactured.

As beautiful as a large sailing area here on the Elbe may be, one cannot quite escape the fascination of this aircraft factory, which after all provides qualified jobs for around 12,500 people in Hamburg. Depending on whether Airbus is about to embark on another cost-cutting programme, as is often the case, there may be more. Shortly after leaving the Rüschkanal in Finkenwerder and entering the Elbe, there are signs on the bank warning of landing aircraft. This is because the Hamburg-Finkenwerder airfield is located here on the site. So Hamburg really does have a second airport on its city territory. Incidentally, in 1967 a Spanish pilot mistook this runway for the one in Hamburg-Fuhlsbüttel and landed his passenger plane in Finkenwerder. It was a narrow escape, and the jet almost fell into the Elbe. The runway was later extended to 3183 metres in April 2006.

But I had visited the plant before: my neighbour worked for Airbus and I visited the plant as a student at an open day. So much high-tech aircraft production in the middle of Hamburg, that impressed me a lot back then. Only the Mühlenberger Loch has lost a lot of ground. Although it is still a beautiful, albeit smaller, area compared to the Mühlenberg in Blankenese.

We continue towards Wedel, still pushed along by the Elbe. Now we are going along the Falkensteiner Ufer. The buildings on the slopes become looser, there are more detached villas instead of houses standing close together. This is also where the "Roman Garden" is hidden in the Elbe slope, a gem that also includes an amphitheatre.

An original spot then comes on the Wittenberg bank: there is one of the few campsites directly on the Elbe that is not hidden behind a dyke. Because the banks of the Elbe are high enough here that dikes are not necessary. In an area with extremely high prices per square metre just outside Hamburg, a campsite is almost an anachronism. "Elbecamp" is the name of the site today. There is a separate zone for tents, which I like. Caravans are pulled onto their sites by the groundsman with a tractor. Because there is Elbe sand everywhere, which could make it difficult for vehicles to manoeuvre. Those who are lucky enough to have rented one of the 45 permanent pitches will be careful not to give it up again: no new pitches have been available for years. But campers who would like to pitch their tent in the suburbs of the big city can warmly recommend this site.

The diesel is humming, we hold our course and continue down the Elbe. Now we pass the somewhat old, large coal-fired power station in Wedel, where a freighter is being unloaded. It's amazing that it's still in operation, but the plant is needed to supply district heating. Then there are the slopes of the Elbe on which the houses of Wedel stand before the land becomes flatter.

If you listen carefully now, you might hear the fanfare from the "Flying Dutchman" by Richard Wagner: "Steuermann, lass die Wacht." This fanfare sounds over from the Schulau ship welcoming system, which also has its loudspeakers pointed at the river. It is a classic Hamburg excursion destination. And even as a child in the seventies, I was fascinated by the ship welcomes, especially since my father worked in the port of Hamburg. I could listen for hours to the "captain" in his glass cabin greeting the ships on the Elbe by microphone, telling them what the ship had loaded and where it was going. To this end, he played a cassette with the national anthem of the flag from which the ship came. Today, this would be a wonderful anachronism: if he still had to put in cassettes, the ones with the anthems of the flags of convenience would probably be pretty worn out, while the cassettes with the German anthem would still be in good shape. Many ships with black-red-gold on their sterns no longer even pass the Elbe here. A nice gag: on a James Last album from the seventies, the famous bandleader recorded the sound of the ship's welcoming system and had "Captain James" wish him a good voyage.

After all, the Schulau Ferry Building has undergone a thorough renovation in recent years, which was also necessary to catapult the excursion restaurant into the modern era. It is now called "The New Schulau Ferry House" and has revamped the kitchen and the menu. Nevertheless, at its core it is of course still an excursion restaurant with a ship's welcoming system, which should give guests a little taste of the big wide world. And what if ... No, we pass the facility unnoticed. No "Helmsman, let down your guard" sounds as we pass the tower with the loudspeakers. But we don't have to, after all we are not going to exotic countries today, but to the marina in Wedel again.

From there, the big, wide world of oceans is open to you again. You can sail back to Scandinavia via the Kiel Canal, but you can also sail down the Elbe to Cuxhaven. Whether you come from the Netherlands or Belgium, from France or Great Britain, the way will take you back to the North Sea here. There is a lot to discover in the Elbe, and the megacity of Hamburg is well worth a visit, whether you combine it with a trip to the Baltic Sea or not. I hope that in this last chapter I have been able to convey to you a little of the fascination of our home district, of the land between the marshes and the Geest, on the great river, the Elbe, in the heart of which lies Hamburg.

ALSO BY
FLORIAN JOHN HANAUER

„A Picture Journey to Haparanda: Sailing the coasts of Scandinavia": A full colour book with photographs from our journeys to the Gulf of Bothnia, the Kattegat and Skagerrak; from Norway to Sweden and Finland.

In German:

„Zwei Hamburger segeln nach Haparanda" German Edition as printed Book, E-Book or Audiobook

„Der Törn vom Haff ins Watt: Eine Segelreise von Berlin nach Bremen" German Edition, printed Book or E-Book

„Vom Öresund zum Oslofjord: Eine Nordlandfahrt unter Segeln", German Edition, printed Book or E-Book

If you liked this book I would be grateful for a review. If you would like to contact me: info@edition-svanen.de